C000243841

TO

LONDON

Signature

2011

HART ROAD
LONDON

Hard Road
to
London

IDRIS EVANS

Published by Steptoes Publishers, Wynnstay Rd., Ruthin. Denbs. LL15 1AS

© Copyright: Idris Evans, 2008

ISBN 978 0 9561878 0 2

The author asserts his moral right under the
Copyright, Designs and Patents Act, 1988
to be identified as author of this work.

All rights reserved. No part of this book may be reproduced,
stored in a retrieval system, or transmitted in any form
or by any means, electronic, electrostatic, magnetic tape, mechanical,
photocopying, recording or otherwise without permission
in writing from the above publishers.

Printed and bound in Wales at
Gomer Press, Llandysul, Ceredigion

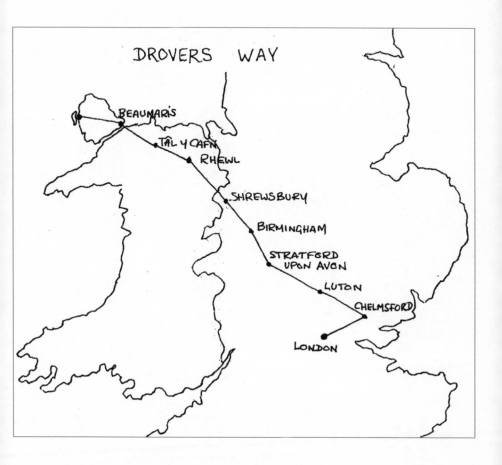

DROVERS WAY

BEAUMAR'S

TAL Y CAFN

RHEWL

SHREWSBURY

BIRMINGHAM

STRATFORD UPON AVON

LUTON

CHELMSFORD

LONDON

1

I was too young to remember much about my Grandfather on my Mothers side but I do know however, that he lost his first wife who was only forty two when she died and that he was left with a Village Post Office to run, four young children and a rambling hill farm that was located on the Northern slopes of the Berwyn mountains on the Denbighshire- Merionethshire border.

My Mother was the eldest child and had to take on the responsibilities of running the home, attending school and becoming the youngest Postmistress in Wales at the age of thirteen.

I was often told by her with some pride, I might add, that my Grandfather was also a 'Porthmon'. A Drover Dealer.

The name did not mean much to me then, except that I knew it was connected to the movement of farm animals over distances to market.

It was to be many years before I was to get involved with this word again.

As the son of a hill farming family, I was much younger than my sister and brothers and was reminded constantly that I was the spoilt one of the family. This I can confirm to be very true, as I always had more or less my own way with most things and the best of everything.

I was growing up at a time when the whole nation was becoming independent and free for the first time in many years. It was post war and cities such as Liverpool and its surrounding towns had suffered greatly from being bombed day and night but they were now getting used to the fact that they could at last visit the open spaces of the countryside. Complete families were getting their first taste of clean fresh air.

The cycle, motor cycle and if you were wealthy the motor car was now to be seen on the public roads for the first time. North Wales being fairly close to both Liverpool and Birkenhead was high on the list of places to visit. It was not uncommon to see the odd motorcycle and sidecar so heavily laden with up to five people plus a dog chugging its way up the narrow lanes searching for a place to pitch a tent for the night.

Camping was becoming increasingly popular, as second hand ex war department tents and equipment were cheap to purchase.

These city folk were now visiting the countryside on a regular basis whether it is for a day, weekend or longer and bringing with them a host of stories, memories and experiences spanning six years of the Second World war. They would tell of how they had all spent what must have seemed endless hours huddled together in miserable, damp and dark bomb shelters and underground stations night after night as the German Luftwaffe did their best to destroy their city and its docks.

These city folk were used to a lifestyle that was alien to us and I remember spending many an evening around an open campfire, mouth open, listening to their sometimes sad, but mostly humorous experiences of everyday life under what must have been extremely difficult and dangerous conditions.

It was now so different, the fear people had for their lives was gone and there was new hope for a brighter and more prosperous future.

For a child who was not accustomed to anything but the freedom of the open countryside and not having had to endure any of the restrictions that had been forced upon these poor people it was difficult for me a country boy to relate to their experiences.

The only restrictions I can remember, was the blackout when every light had to be covered, all windows had to have heavy black curtains fitted to make sure not even a flicker could be seen from the outside and vehicles had to have special covers over the lights to make sure they could not be seen from the sky.

We as a farming family always had an abundance of fresh food so we never suffered from the rationing that was in force throughout the country. Because of the shortage of essential fresh foods, it did mean we became instant friends with people that we did not really know too well.

It was not unknown for the local Police sergeant to visit us under the cover of darkness on the pretext that it was official business that needed seeing to. As far as I can remember, nothing 'official' was ever discussed apart from chapel business, as he was a deacon with my father in the local Congregational Welsh chapel. On completing discussions of a more heavenly nature, he would slip away into the night with the odd dozen eggs and a piece of ham hidden discretely under his cape.

What we did see was the influence of the tractor as motive power for the first time. Great emphasis was now being placed on the home production of crops making the effort of the farmer much more concentrated. Feeding the nation was of prime importance, but apart from having to conform to the blackout law, little else had changed during the whole of the war for us farming folk.

As soon as war ended, the day came when I had to leave the confines and security of the farm and its animals for that very first day at the local infant's school. A major step for any child but for me an experience I have tried to forget ever since.

From that very first moment I stepped into the classroom with its smells of chalk and ink and coke that burned on the pot- bellied stove, I took an instant dislike to the whole thing and knew there and then it was not for me. Probably the freedom I had enjoyed up to this point did not make it any easier as I was not used to rules or having to conform to the many restraints that went with being a pupil in a school.

Although my background sounds idyllic, it was in many ways a lonely childhood. As I was the youngest by some twelve years, loneliness I suppose was inevitable, my brothers and sister were of another generation and when you live some distance away from towns and other families you can't just pop out of the front door to play and make friends. Other children had to be delivered to you or if you were lucky enough to be invited to someone's home then you had to be taken and it was a major undertaking for any parent in those days, as transport was not too plentiful and the motor car far beyond the financial reach of most people.

Because most children had made friends long before the start of school, this was a problem for me as I always seemed to be the stranger, the one on the outside so to speak. This was to cause me some discomfort in the early stages and was probably the reason why I came to rely heavily on a set of well- rehearsed excuses why I should not go to school.

Illness was my number one excuse and I became quite expert at feigning the symptoms of some rather unusual complaints.

Eventually I started to run low on acceptable reasons why I should be kept at home.

My lack of attendance was starting to show at school and I was getting well behind the rest of the class in academic achievement. My stupid escapades were not helping me bond with other classmates or the teachers both of whom had shown I must confess a great degree of tolerance over many months. My spasmodic attendance certainly did not help me cope very well with the end of term tests.

It became obvious to my parents that I was not going to settle and I was eventually sent, very much against my will to a Boys Boarding School not too far away, but far enough to make it more difficult for me to escape.

From the very first day, I was again determined not to stay in this dreadful establishment. This was worse, much worse, this was 'Tom Brown's schooldays' in real life, a large grey miserable cold building with Dickensian style teachers and attitudes, with rules that would not have been out of place in the most gruesome of prisons.

It operated a strict rule of secrecy that was never to be broken. If you did break it, life would become intolerable, a living hell on earth.

Local pupils were never really accepted into this closed society as most of the poor souls attending this institution came from all corners of the world and were often abandoned by their parents,

The masters regarded it as character building; they believed that if you were able to survive on your own under what can only be described as unsavoury conditions that this would set you up for whatever the world was to throw at you during your future life. This meant that the boys who boarded soon built an association with one another that was not easily penetrated by a newcomer, so it always took some time to be accepted. Perhaps in my case, I did not give it a chance and probably never did try hard enough.

It was the freedom of the land and the buzz of the Cattle Markets and Horse Fairs that drew me like a moth to a light.

That was the world I knew well and felt most comfortable in. I would use any and every excuse under the sun to be there mingling with the crowds and soaking up the incredible atmosphere that was always present.

The monthly horse sales now a thing of the past. These occasions were so full of atmosphere with as much of a mixture of horses as of people. I remember the Romany's with their colourful caravans and bareback riding at speed through the gathered throng of potential buyers.

When I look back on those heady days and bask in the memories, I remember so much.

A question I was frequently asked was,

Not in school today then? Not feeling well are we?

My answer was always the same,

No!

Nothing else

Just No.

I found it was always better to keep the answer short and to the point.

Being in the company of my eldest brother on these memorable occasions he would often reply on my behalf saying. 'This young man is being educated in the University of Life'. He was probably right because it was a fantastic education, but it still didn't help me much when I had to face those dreaded school exam papers later on.

During these, I am ashamed to admit too regular visits I found myself engulfed by a fascinating mix of the human race. Men who left an overriding impression on me and I am sure contributed greatly to my development later on in life.

These were ordinary country folk but with bright colourful personalities, most of them had survived on their wits and their cunning ways, for times had been extremely hard for many of them.

They taught me what life was all about and how situations however difficult they seemed to be at the time, could often be turned into an advantage, these were the original optimists. Survival was always pretty high on their list and they seemed to be masters at it.

Over the years, I had learned many things.

Probably the main one was to listen and keep the mouth shut and if possible, work out what others were thinking before being tempted to make any comment or judgment.

I had to learn this message from a very early age as my family were from a long line of Cattle and Horse Dealers, as you can imagine an interesting and potent mix.

Sadly it also meant you could never really call anything your own, everything seemed to be just on loan to you, always with a price on it and there to be sold.

As a child I could never really build up a relationship with any pet as I could be relieved of it at any time, this resulted in many a tear being shed over the years when I saw my favourite dog or horse being taken away by some stranger, never to be seen again.

This is why I suppose I built up a wonderful and lasting relationship with a most unusual pet for a farmer's son, a tortoise called Noddy.

Nobody wanted to buy a tortoise so I had him until he died of old age.

Nevertheless, things always moved on, next day, next week, something else would capture my attention and affection and the whole cycle would start again.

That was life as it had been for many a year and it was not likely to change for the foreseeable future.

As part of this dealing family, I was made aware very early on that one wrong word in the wrong place and in front of a potential buyer could mean disaster, the difference between a sale and no sale. Success or failure.

I had been told clearly on more than one occasion, just listen and say nothing.

Another lesson I will carry with me all my life.

The secret of success or should I say survival in the world of dealing is, you have to buy well and sell very well and quickly. The idea being that you turn your capital over as many times as possible in the shortest time and hopefully make a small profit on each occasion.

This formula did not work every time, in fact not often enough but it was something a good dealer always kept his eye on at all times and tried hard to achieve.

If you happened to be the purchaser of an animal then you had to negotiate the best possible price but only after you had carefully checked the condition as there was always the fear that there may be some concealed problem, one that could result in early mortality.

Horses, were always sold with the term, 'Sound in Wind and limb'. This I suppose meant the animal should be fit and healthy, but sadly this was not always the case as they were often propped up for sale with some concoction that would only last to stimulate the poor animal's outward appearance and keep it on its feet until you got it home. In those days there were no fair trading laws to protect you, it was up to your judgement and your responsibility, it would be almost impossible to get your money back if it died, so it would be a 'Dead loss'.

The inspection of an animals mouth was always the best method of checking its overall condition as this would reveal its general health and its true age, all this being revealed by its teeth.

The term 'Buyer Beware' when buying or selling anything has never left me and never will. On too many occasions, we were landed with what turned out to be a sad case, the reason being that we took someone's word as gospel.

There is a very old saying, you always have to learn the hard way and I have found there are no exceptions to this important rule.

It was during my regular visits to the various markets, these 'Pits of Wits' that I would regularly meet and mix with the local 'Porthmyn', (Drovers).

These were usually small farmers, who supplemented their meagre incomes with part time droving, walking animals from outlying farms on a journey of anything from twenty to thirty miles to the local markets.

Its strange how habits have changed over the years and what sticks in your memory. For me of all things, was the habit they all seemed to eagerly participate in and that was chewing tobacco and spitting.

It was almost a requirement of the trade.

They believed that if you were to survive the rigours of the open road you had to chew a lump of 'bacci.'

I was always told it helped to prevent the swallowing of dust and other unmentionables that were always present as a result of moving live animals along the rough and dirty country roads, as most of these highways were constructed of compressed soil and crushed stone.

It must have worked, because to me they all seemed to have withstood the passing of the years very well.

They were also expert whistlers, an art that seems to have gone with the passing of time; they would merrily whistle a wide mixture of tunes from traditional Welsh airs to famous hymns. Today I can only think of one person I know that carries on this practice. What a shame because I always felt the people who whistled always seemed to be happy and contented.

I remember on one cold, wet miserable morning being offered a cut of 'Twist' this was the trademark of what seemed to be the most popular brand of tobacco to chew at the time.

The reason I was given it was because I made the fatal mistake of complaining that I had toothache.

A small chunk of Bacci was immediately offered with the instruction to press it down hard on the offending tooth, I was told this would take the pain away and the effect would last until I could at least get to a dentist.

I was presented with it still stuck to the blade of a well worn and seriously stained penknife, what this instrument had been used for in the past I dread to think but reluctantly I accepted it and thrust this brown mass into my mouth holding it down on the offending tooth before dwelling too much on the history of the tobacco or the knife.

It worked!

Within minutes, I was pain free. A miracle!

Most of these cattlemen carried a roll of this tobacco in their waistcoat pocket; it was dark brown in colour, the thickness of a pencil and coiled like a rope. As they felt the urge to replenish what they had been, chewing for some hours a new piece would be cut off and thrust between the recipients dribbling lips.

You could see it gave instant pleasure and judging by the dreadful stains on their teeth, must have acted as some sort of permanent painkiller with built in protection against infection of the gums; otherwise, I am sure they would all have been toothless.

You could always identify a 'bacci' chewer as they always had the tell tale signs, brown stains running from the mouth and down both sides of the chin.

These characters were also experts at the dubious art of spitting.

Once those sparkling jewelled eyes, which were nearly always under the shelter of well-grown bushy eyebrows logged onto a target, they would spit with the velocity and accuracy of a bullet.

Although an unacceptable practice today spitting was practiced until relatively recently, by both men and women whatever their social standing within the community.

In years gone by the spittoon was an essential piece of equipment in virtually every alehouse and many a home. For the un initiated this was a cylindrical vessel normally in brass or copper with a hole some three inches in diameter in the top of the lid, it was always placed reasonably close to the fireplace presumably because if the target was missed, the remains would then be absorbed by the fire.

Spitting competitions were common in the majority of Public houses and bets would often be taken to see who was the most accurate at a predetermined distance.

Imagine having the splendid title of Spitting Champion of the County.

The tradition of Luck money within the farming fraternity has been in existence for centuries and religiously takes place even today when any item is sold.

To describe this formality is not easy and at first can seem complicated, but the end result seems to be to the satisfaction of everyone.

The arrangement is as follows.

As soon as the final price of a deal is agreed, both participants shake the hand. To seal the deal the seller always spits on his own hand before he shakes the hand of the buyer. Once the buyer has paid his dues, a token amount of money is given back from the seller to the buyer. This is known as 'Luck Money'

It is a token of the seller's pleasure and faith in the deal and being a way of making sure the deal will be blessed with. 'Good luck'.

Even today with emphasis on Health and Safety this practice still takes place in rural areas and is still very much part of country life.

As far as I was concerned, the luck was always mine because I ended up with the money in my pocket for sweets.

This most unhygienic practice has been in existence for hundreds of years and I have witnessed many transactions but I can honestly say, I have never met anyone who suffered any illness directly attributable to this practice.

By studying and witnessing the art of Dealing, it was to stand me in good stead for the rest of my life, as I eventually became a Dealer myself.

Not in animals, but in things of a more general nature.

2

Because of my chosen destiny I decided some years ago to buy a house in the beautiful Vale of Clwyd in the county of Denbighshire and I was drawn to a property in the tranquil village of Rhewl, a small but interesting gathering of houses situated a mile or so to the West of the picturesque Mediaeval Market Town of Ruthin.

The name Rhewl translated into English means Highway or Thoroughfare and this village although I didn't realise it at the time was to play a very important part in one of the most exiting quests I have ever undertaken.

Ruthin was burned to the ground in 1401 but was soon rebuilt and today stands as it has done since those days of yore on a hill and is a majestic reminder of its chequered past with its Elizabethan style half timbered and dressed stone houses and its medieval castle in red sandstone glistening in the regular rays of sunshine that this valley seems to enjoy throughout the year.

Owain Glyndwr became the last true Prince of Wales. He was actually born in South Wales but his family owned two large estates one at Rhug near the town of Corwen on the banks of the river Dee where they spent the winter months and Sycharth near the village of Llansilin in Southern Denbighshire where they would enjoy their summers. Both places were indicative of a family that had the trappings of wealth and influence. The latter house was the larger of the two being an opulent mansion of motte and bailey design and construction, surrounded with a water-filled moat. It also supported some very unusual architectural features for the times, in the form of large chimneys to take out the smoke and a tiled roof

Rare exotic birds and animals roamed the extensive gardens, which made this residence unique within Wales. It was a very suitable residence for a large family of wealth and royal connection. Its reputation for the magnificence of its festive board and warm welcome meant it became well known throughout the Principality and beyond ensuring it was always on the list of many a hungry and tired traveller.

Owain was a man who was to change the face of Wales forever.

He was a direct descendent of the two Royal households in the Principality, his Father from the lands of Gwynedd and Powys and his Mother from Deheubarth in the South.

He spoke Welsh, English and Latin fluently and furthered his education in the Inns of London becoming a brilliant lawyer. Highly regarded within society and Royal circles but more interested in the military he pledged his allegiance to the King of England and fought in many a battle on the Kings side.

On his eventual return to his lands in Wales there were some who regarded him as a traitor as he had sided with the English crown others saw him as a threat. One such person being Lord Reginald De Grey of Castell Coch (Ruthin Castle)who had been installed by the crown to report any unease with the Welsh.

The two had once been good friends fighting side by side but it was de Grey who now betrayed him. He intentionally failed to inform Owain that an instruction had been received directly from the King requesting Owain to attend a meeting and to send an attachment of his best bowmen to assist the knights in battle. At the same time De Grey had stolen some of Owain's land.

These two actions were to cost De Grey dearly as neither was appreciated by this intelligent dynamic and much loved Welshman.

Because the Royal directive was never received by Owain and his men never sent, it was looked upon as an act of treason by the King.

Therefore, instructions were duly sent to De Grey for Owain and his men to be captured and imprisoned forthwith.

On secretly receiving knowledge of this instruction and knowing there would be a price on his head, Owain gathered a number of his trusted men to his side and after pondering throughout the night at his home at Sycharth, raised his standard and rode under the cover of darkness into the town of Ruthin. After making sure all houses had been cleared of their occupants, he set fire to most of the buildings surrounding the castle.

This was his act of revenge against De Grey and the marcher lords who were now introducing crippling taxes on the Welsh nation in order to pay for the Hundred Years War.

This severe act was to set this fiery young warrior on a journey that was to rewrite the history of the nation.

Owain was pronounced Prince of Wales at a ceremony that took place in the small village of Glyndyfrdwy on the banks of the river Dee five miles east of his residence at Rhug, Corwen and it was on this occasion that he took on the name Owain Glyndwr which means 'Owain of the valley of the Dee'

This new and much loved leader set off on a journey that was to stir the nation into revolt against England and as he went from North to South, was able to gain formidable support from all factions of society. Academics in London together with ordinary folk in employment over the border had heard of the uprising and were now flocking home to join the new cause, as confidence grew stronger with every new day. Owain's natural leadership and his ability and experience as a fighter were becoming well known throughout the country. He was using guerrilla tactics not known before and this was proving very successful against the enemy. Camouflage, surprise attacks and picking off small numbers of the opposition at one time then disappearing quickly into the undergrowth was having tremendous success, as it was a method of fighting the English soldiers were not used to and found difficult to counteract. They were not efficient in the mountains of Wales; they had been trained to fight with heavy armour in the open and mostly on flat ground.

Prior to this Ruthin had enjoyed a peaceful existence and had built up an enviable reputation as an important trading centre and Market Town dealing in rare precious commodities such as gold, silver, silks and spices. It was a merchant's town in every sense of the word.

It catered too for the people who made a living from the land, boasting vibrant Cattle and Horse Fairs both sealed with Royal Charters.

Over the years the thick forests had been cleared to make way for development in agriculture, farming practices were now taking hold the fertile land and the temperate climate meant there was an abundance of good harvests. Crops were easily grown and casual labour readily available with local hiring fairs full of young men offering their services to anyone who cared to employ them on a seasonal or permanent basis.

The surrounding areas of mixed hard woods were being felled at a considerable rate with newly felled oak being in great demand by the many ship builders on the coasts of Wales and England. Local builders were now busy building new dwellings and modifying existing ones around the area.

Apart from oak, ash was much in demand for the manufacturing of carts, traps, the alders from the wet lands of the valley floor were used for making furniture and the soles of clogs, young hazel was ideal for wattle and daub, and the sycamore was a favourite for kitchen and dairy utensils. All these timbers were on hand and in abundance.

3

Today Rhewl is still a small village but with a vibrant community of both local Welsh speakers and English newcomers, many of whom struggle to learn the language with others just happy to play their part in the village activities.

The surrounding area today is a patchwork quilt of large productive farms where cultivation and stock breeding go hand in hand, scattered dwellings pepper the landscape and meandering through the floor of the valley is a major trunk road which winds its way from south east to north west connecting the rural areas to the coast. The river Clywedog still ambles its way as it has done for many thousands of years toward

the sea and soon meets up with another river, the Clwyd to become a much larger force.

The hub of the community is an Inn called the 'Drovers Arms'. Yes and there is still a house called 'Buarthau.'

The Inn today is a well-known watering hole for the thirsty and a supplier of good country food for the hungry. Until recently, it had the shelter of Scots Pine trees around its perimeter but sadly someone in their wisdom decided to cut them down obviously not realising how important they were as a record of its ancient connection with the past.

However, our new home was to hold the key to a fascinating historical journey that was to expose a treasure chest of history.

Facts that had been hidden for many a year were now about to be exposed for the very first time.

Out of the mists of time came a magical story that was to open up a new and exiting world for me and I have been fortunate that I have been able to share this story many times through the talks I have given on this subject to various societies over the past few years.

Almost by accident, I realised that I had stumbled on one of the most important pieces of history relating to a tradition that had contributed more than any other to the development of Wales and its people and that was 'Droving'.

The clue became obvious by looking at the name of the house, Buarthau. Translated into English it means 'Yards' or 'Enclosures'. The word Buarth the singular, Buarthau, the plural.

You will not find too many dwellings with this name but the ones you do come across are always close to roads where the cattle Drovers travelled or rested and are a certain indicator of an association with the walking and the safekeeping of animals during their journey to the South.

I had just taken to a new hobby at this time. Metal detecting!

This was something I had wanted to do for many years but never had the time.

Now I had an opportunity to take up what I thought would be a rewarding pastime. I invested in a reasonably good second hand detector that appeared on inspection to be in excellent condition and was told by the owner that he had experienced many hours of pleasure with some reasonable success. He did point out after the deal had been completed that he couldn't find the instruction book but that it would not be a problem as the machine was very simple to operate and that I would get used to it very quickly. After a brief demonstration and taking the mans word for it I set off for home with great haste.

I later learned to my cost that the instruction book is the most important part of the equipment.

I now know why it was so reasonably priced and why he accepted my offer so quickly. Without the book, it was virtually useless. There were so many knobs, switches and dials to be read together with a discriminator facility. What on earth was a discriminator I asked myself, I eventually took it to mean that it would discriminate between detecting rubbish and something that was worth recovering. The only way to see if it worked was to try it out on the land and see what happened.

Attempting to fathom the intricacies of this contraption took longer than I had anticipated and not being blessed with an abundance of patience, I became extremely frustrated. Working things out logically is not my forte so I set off in pursuit of fortune ill equipped, ignorant and impatient.

Headphones on head, detector in hand which to the uninitiated at first glance resembles a broom handle with a frying pan attached to the one end, a trowel to assist with the digging, wellies on the feet I was off like a racing greyhound released from the starting trap.

The idea of detecting being if and when you pass what is called in the trade the head (That is the piece that looks like a frying pan) over or near a metal object it emits a signal through wires to the headphones. It was important, I was told, to wear headphones because it was then possible to pick up the weakest of signals and it is the weakest signal that reveals the best results. This I presumed meant that you were not supposed to miss a single article.

The sound you are anxiously waiting to hear is a long note almost like the squeal of an unhappy pig. Lo and behold, I encountered my very first squeal within seconds of placing the round bit close to the ground.

My quest for fortune was truly launched. A long solid eeeeh . . . filled both my ears.

With trowel gripped tightly, I started to dig like someone who had only minutes to live and that my whole future was going to be determined within the next few seconds. This I thought could be a life changing experience!

Gold bullion! A Roman hoard! Celtic Gold bangle maybe? Ok, Silver would do.

After a few minutes digging which I must confess seemed much longer there was a neat round hole in the ground about twelve inches deep and six inches across but not a single coin or artefact to be seen.

You are advised by the professionals not to make any unnecessary mess and to stack the soil from the hole in such a way that it can be easily put back, this unwritten rule is supposedly to save animosity and conflict between you and a landowner.

It didn't matter at this precise moment because I was still on our own land but later as my search area was to expand onto our neighbour's fields it was an important piece of etiquette to remember as I did not want to create any ill feeling between me and my new neighbours.

After exerting a tremendous amount of energy, well I thought it was a lot as I am not the fittest man on the planet; I began to feel rather dejected, as I had absolutely nothing to show for my efforts.

Another step another squeal!

Again digging furiously I became aware that blisters were now starting to show on my fingers making it not only a fruitless experience but a painful one too. Another step and yes you've guessed it, the same result, absolutely nothing.

This futile activity went on for some considerable time and disappointment was now starting to show, my enthusiasm was waning quickly. I could not understand why I was getting a good strong signal and yet my pockets were absolutely empty.

At this stage, I was definitely not impressed and I was ready to throw the whole contraption into the river. I had worked hard over the last hour and nothing to show for my efforts not even a rusty nail.

Looking back over what turned out to be some considerable distance the mounds of rejected earth were now becoming reminiscent of a vigorous mole and I was now completely dejected.

It was while I was sitting on the grass and pondering over my disappointing results that I took a moment to gather my thoughts and then suddenly realised with some embarrassment that I had found the cause of my problem

The wellie's I was wearing had steel toecaps!

Every time my foot went within close proximity of the search head, it transmitted information that under normal circumstances would be useful. All it did to me was to confirm what was now obvious.

I was to learn very quickly from this miserable experience and after contacting a friend who was an experienced detectorist for his advice and guidance; I got the hang of it and did eventually start finding the odd nail and other bits of rubbish that had been discarded over the years.

Then on a beautiful warm summers evening I heard a tone in my ears that I had not heard before, this one was definitely different.

I felt my heart start to beat faster and faster somehow; I just knew that I was onto something good this time. What happened next was to become a magical experience.

I started to find treasure! Well, it was treasure to me.

It wasn't a hoard of gold coins or precious artefacts from some forgotten civilisation but I did start to find a reasonable amount of silver and copper coins.

The earliest date I could decipher was 1400 and something, some looked much older but sadly they were too corroded for me to be able to read any dates. I was also finding buckles, buttons and other pieces of metal, which with a vivid imagination, which I do possess incidentally, could be anything, you wanted them to be.

There was however, one coin that was turning up at fairly regular intervals, which I eventually discovered to be the 'Anglesey Penny' with its partner, the Halfpenny.

These were heavy copper coins much larger than a traditional penny and much thicker. The penny measured one and a half inches across and the halfpenny slightly smaller.

As I desperately rubbed the dirt off my first example it revealed some very interesting and fascinating identification marks.

On the one side, it had what appeared to be a 'Druids head' surrounded by oak leaves. On the obverse, large letters in a copperplate style 'P.M.Co. 1787.' Around the edge was inscribed 'We Promise to pay the Bearer on demand in Liverpool, Anglesey and London.

It was these coins that set me off on a fascinating journey of discovery and was to give me endless hours of pleasure researching their source. These were coins or tokens produced by a Thomas Williams who owned the Parys copper mine at Amlwch on the Northern tip of the Isle of Anglesey hence P.M.Co Parys Mining Company. He was also known in his day as the copper king of the world and had amassed a large fortune out of this mineral. Copper had been mined from this site before the Roman occupation, but it was Thomas Williams who exploited its potential.

Being probably one of the most astute businessmen of his time, he had persuaded the drovers to use his coins as payment at the many Inns and resting places on their journey South. This would spare them having to carry more gold coins than was needed as robbery during the journey was of major concern. Because these were mere tokens and not coins of the realm they were of no value to a highwayman or anyone else apart from the appointed few and therefore safe for the drovers to carry.

A substantial amount of these coins was produced in fact there were over twelve and a half million equating to two hundred and fifty tons in circulation at one time making a total value at the time of £340.000. Quite a substantial amount of money in the eighteenth century.

The copper would be smelted and formed into sheets at Amlwch and then transported on board his own ships to dock at Greenfield on the North Wales coast a journey of some sixty nautical miles to the East. Then it would be transported by road to Holywell in Flintshire where he owned an industrial complex and a substantial area of land. Here he took advantage of a good supply of fast moving water and installed a water hammer, which further fettled the copper into more manageable sections. The blank discs would then be stamped out from the fashioned copper into the two sizes he required for his coins. These were then sent by road to his Birmingham factory to have the details added to both sides. He at this time formed a partnership with a

Mathew Boulton with a view to supplying coins of the realm, which sadly for him never materialised. He was tricked and out manoeuvred by his so-called close friend and duly lost the contract.

It is not absolutely certain why he chose a druids head to be placed on the one side of the coin but some believe it was because he actually lived on the banks of the Menai straights opposite the site of the last stand of the Welsh Druids against the Romans. The Welsh Druids were looked upon as the cruellest people the Romans had ever encountered owing to the fact that they still practiced human sacrifice.

Whatever Thomas Williams's reason for choosing this profile makes these coins very impressive and today a true collector's item.

4

Buarthau, was located just off the main road between Ruthin and Denbigh on the banks of the river Clywedog. A river that started as a trickle way up in the hills above the vale but had gradually carved its way as it gathered momentum over millennia through limestone rock and in doing so had left a deep gorge leaving and an effect resembling organ pipes in a cathedral, in other places it had hewn an intricate pattern that looked like lace in a shawl out of this hard stone. This aggressive rush of water was eventually to become calmer as it meandered through the flat lands of the valley on its way to the sea.

In the past, our dwelling had been of some considerable acreage but now only a relatively large mature garden survived extending gracefully down to the banks of this magnificent river.

The building itself was built of dressed limestone a commodity that was on hand and plentiful. Although the roof was now of slate there were signs that the second story had been added at a much later date probably around the sixteen hundreds and that the original dwelling would have been a single storey with a simple thatched covering.

The walls were some three feet thick with the original small windows that let in a limited amount of daylight; this meant the house was always warm in winter and cool in summer.

Careful celestial observation by the original builders made sure that the position of the house would face East, Southeast. This was to gain maximum exposure to the sun from dawn to dusk in both summer and winter.

There were some obvious signs that other alterations had taken place over the past centuries especially to the interior. The room that would have been the centre of the building and the only one to have a fire at that time was to reveal five fireplaces; each built one in front of the other.

This proved to be a fascinating discovery as it gave us an on the spot insight into the interior fashions of the various periods of the past.

On carefully removing the final one, we uncovered an unusually large inglenook with small recesses let into the stone at various heights from the floor. These would have been created to keep various articles dry such as candles, kindling for the fire and the most important commodity of all salt, as this was required for a number of different reasons apart from being used to preserve meat it was also used to pay wages and this is where the word salary came from.

At the one end was a much larger opening, which accommodated the bread oven as bread, was always made on the premises using the heat of the fire.

All this was under a large blackened oak beam spanning some fifteen feet in length and still bearing many a scorch mark left from candles that had been used to light an otherwise dark and smoky room.

The candleholders would have been simple metal spikes with a holder on one end and a sharp point on the other; these would be rammed into the beam wherever light was needed. The candles themselves would be made from local rushes gathered from the wet fields at higher ground known in welsh as 'Ffriddoedd' The harvested rush would be brought down in late summer, cut into suitable lengths and hung up to be dried. In early Autumn, special nights were arranged within the community to cut and strip the rush, these nights were known as 'Pilnos' Once stripped they would be dipped into animal fats allowed to dry and harden and stored until they were required, these were to become the forerunners of our modern candle.

Most of the timbers that had been used to accommodate a second storey were showing identical burn marks, the reason being that it was common practice to incorporate well-seasoned beams reclaimed from old ships.

Because of the close proximity to ship builders along the length of the North Wales coast and Liverpool, new timbers were being delivered and reclaimed beams from ships no longer deemed seaworthy were willingly sold as scrap and purchased by local builders. As most of the timbers would have been removed from below deck they came complete with burn marks already on them. This would be as a result of sailors having to go below deck to areas of the ship that would have been in total darkness, they would have used similar metal spikes and candle holders to light up an otherwise dark and dingy area.

Exposing the inglenook was a most filthy and time-consuming operation, removing generations of loose material such as stones, soot, lime, dust and grime made regular visits to inhale clean fresh air essential. The dust caused us the greatest problem throughout our renovations.

I remember seeing a play many years ago called 'The Roses of Eyam'. A true storey of how the spores of the Plague could survive in dust for hundreds of years. If it was true, then it was not good news.

It told of the tragic story of the people of Eyam, a small village in the hills of Derbyshire where virtually the whole population had been wiped out by the plague, this having been brought up from London in second hand clothes which were being sold to the local inhabitants but the clothes contained the spores of the London plague. It is from this sad story that we get the nursery rhyme Ring a Ring a Roses. The effect of the plague produced rings on the faces of the inhabitants similar to the petals of a rose. Even to this very day the residents of this most picturesque village will not dig their gardens for fear that the spores still remain in the soil.

Bearing this in mind and the fact that the Plague had virtually wiped out the town of Ruthin and the surrounding area on three different occasions, I was worried.

Needless to say, we all survived!

The floor of the hearth at the base of the chimney was bare earth but with signs that the fire had always burned at ground level and not in a basket. This presumably would have radiated heat from the fire much more efficiently.

Looking upward through the chimney, you could see the sky, which meant that the smoke would have ascended without any form of restriction. Very easy to send a young child up to clean the chimney but wet winter nights could be another story.

One could easily imagine the hundreds of characters that had sat over the years around this hearth with ale in hand and relating endless stories of the past whether they be fact or fiction it probably didn't matter too much.

Dancing to the fiddler and the harp, the singing of traditional songs, drinking and the endless hours of sheer pleasure in the company of friends, all this within these ancient walls. If only these walls could speak.

Even the planked elm doors with their blacksmith fashioned metalwork had been added to by some twelve inches indicating people had grown taller over the years

Underneath the floorboards we found a thick layer of crushed glass, this we were told was to keep vermin at bay and possibly to act as a form of primitive insulation.

The interior dividing walls were made of wattle and daub, wattle being hazel sticks weaved in the same way as in a basket, then wet mud thrown at them and smoothed off which then became the daub. These panels were then encased within vertical and horizontal oak beams held together with wooden pegs.

It was obvious looking at the exterior that the locking stone at the base of the chimney was still in place this was used to lock the thatch to the stonework.

Our intention was always to renovate the property with feeling and to take it back as near as we could to its original character, keeping as many of the original features as we possibly could.

It was decided before we did any more exposing and possible damage, that we contact our local Archives and to enlist the advice of the local Archivist. We felt it was advisable to seek professional help at this early stage, as one mistake could be detrimental to the overall result.

Fortunately, Ruthin has a very comprehensive archive department and they were able to offer us a multitude of facts and interesting pieces of information regarding our home that otherwise we would never have discovered.

The archivist proved to be a very pleasant and learned fellow and helped us wade our way through the history of this fascinating house in some detail.

He informed us among other things that the previous name of the house was 'Plas Cynwrig.'

This was completely different to the name we had proudly displayed on a wrought iron plaque at the entrance of the long oak lined drive, but it immediately captured our interest.

It had been changed to 'Buarthau' he said some time in its distant past probably around 1600 and had been anglicised probably within the last two hundred years to 'Buarthe.' He also told us that there had been a dwelling on this site since the thirteenth century.

Nevertheless, who was this fellow Cynwrig I asked?

Plas was easily translated. In English, it is Hall. So it was originally Cynwrig's Hall. Or to be precise the Hall of Cynwrig.

Cynwrig I was told was a direct descendent of Llewellyn ap Iorweth who in turn was a descendent of Llewellyn the Great.

Llewellyn the Great was born 1173 died in 1201. The greatest Prince in all Wales. A true Princes of Wales!

The sad story of his dog Gelert is still remembered today.

Whether it be fact or fiction I think it is important that it be told to our children and to future generations, I therefore make no apologies for relating this story once again.

Llewellyn had a favourite hunting hound named Gelert. His father-in-law, King John, had given it to him.

The dog was as gentle as a lamb at home but a lion in the chase. One day Llewellyn prepared for the hunt and blew his horn in front of his castle. All his other dogs came to the call but Gelert never answered it. So he blew a louder blast and called Gelert by name but still the hound did not come. At last, Prince Llewellyn could wait any longer and went off to the hunt without his favourite dog.

Hunting that day was poor because he did not have Gelert the swiftest and boldest of them all. He turned back in a rage to his castle and as he came to the gate who should he see but Gelert coming out bounding to meet him. However, when the hound came near him the Prince was startled to see that his lips and fangs were dripping with blood. The dog crouched down at his feet as if surprised or afraid at the way his master greeted him.

Prince Llewellyn had a little son a year old with whom Gelert used to play. A terrible thought crossed the Prince's mind that made him rush to the child's nursery. The nearer he came the more blood and disorder he found about the rooms. He rushed into it and found the child's cradle overturned and covered in blood.

The Prince grew more and more terrified at what he might find and searched for his son and heir everywhere. He failed to find the child but there were signs of some terrible conflict in which much blood had been shed.

He felt sure the dog had attacked the child and shouted at Gelert "Monster, thou hast devoured my child" He drew his sword and plunged it into the side of the hound that fell to the ground with a deep yell and still gazing into his master's eyes.

As Gelert gave his last dying yell, a little child's cry answered it from beneath the upturned cradle and there Llewellyn found his child unharmed and just awakening from sleep. Beside him lay the body of a great wolf torn to pieces and covered in blood.

Too late, Llewellyn now learned what had happened while he was away.

Gelert had stayed behind to guard the child and had fought and slain the wolf that had tried to destroy Llewellyn's heir.

In vein, Llewellyn tried to bring his faithful dog back to life but to no avail.

He buried him in pasture just outside the castle walls within sight of that great mountain, Snowdon where every passer by might see his grave. Today a village stands on that spot and it is called Beddgelert. (Celert's Grave). An everlasting reminder to all who visit this most beautiful part of Wales.

5

Cynwrig, Llewellyn's descendent lived at Plas Cynwrig or Buarthau and involved himself in frequent battles against the English. He participated in one under the banner of his great friend Owain Glyndwr; this was on the banks of the river Dee above Corwen an area the new Prince of Wales knew well for he was brought up on the family estate at Rhug on the outskirts of the town and as a child had ridden with his faithful dog Cabbal by his side over every inch of this area, so he knew this terrain intimately.

He would also have worked out the best place to instigate an attack against the enemy, an area that would give him an advantage and he chose it carefully.

The weather proved to be in Owain's favour on that fateful day for it had been extremely wet and cold for some days.

The English soldiers had been forced by their leaders to march with heavy cumbersome armour through extremely muddy conditions and needing to climb the mighty Berwyn mountain range with little or no food and with the weather against them, they arrived at the battle location very wet, tired, hungry and dejected, a condition the Welsh immediately took advantage of forcing them to retreat. In doing so, the English were to suffer heavy losses but not before they captured Owain's friend, 'Cynwrig'.

He was taken hostage to be used as a ransom or exchange for some notable Englishman that had been taken by the Welsh in some previous battle. This was normal practice by both sides at the time.

What immediately took place then is pure conjecture, but what is known is that poor Cynwrig was incarcerated in Shrewsbury Gaol. His captors not receiving any communication from the Welsh went ahead with a cruel punishment. They extracted his eyes. Apparently, this was the norm in those dim and distant days.

Alas! He did have a choice. Either the eyes out. Or Castration.

He went for the eyes! Presumably the other would have brought uncontrollable tears to his eyes anyway!

The house that this poor man once lived in, the finding of the Anglesey pennies in some quantity, the name of the village Rhewl, (Highway or thoroughfare in English). The Drovers Arms public house on the side of the main road just across the field and the proximity of the river Clywedog to our house, the finding of other coins and artefacts led me to believe there had been a serious amount of activity at this location spread over a great number of years by people who could afford to loose money without worrying too much about it and on a regular basis.

I eventually proved this to be fact.

My quest took me to the furthest reaches of Anglesey. To discover a small band of men known as 'Porthmyn Mon.' the Anglesey Drovers.

Our little village I discovered, had played a major role in the journey of these Anglesey men on their long and arduous journey droving wild Welsh cattle (Runts) aged between eighteen months and three years of age to the lucrative Markets of England and in particular the Great City of London.

It was a three hundred mile trip over some of the most difficult and dangerous terrain in the United Kingdom.

Porthmyn Mon, I discovered were the best of the best, the crème de la crème in the of art of Droving.

The skills they had perfected acted as a milestone to the rest of the Droving fraternity.

Classified as an art and perfected over a thousand years it was faithfully guarded by the few and handed down from one generation to another but always kept within the family.

During the reign of Elizabeth 1st, Droving had become a licensed profession with very serious consequences if the rules were abused or broken.

You had to display your licence plate at all times while droving and this was in the form of a circular metal badge worn on the left arm between the elbow and the shoulder that contained your name and licence number, date and place of issue.

To qualify for this valued document you had to be Male, over the age of thirty, Married and a landowner. This meant you had to have substantial assets and immediately eliminated the undesirable characters who in the past had given the art of droving a bad name by defrauding the people who had entrusted them with what would amount to a substantial part of their annual income and who never returned with the monies owed.

This was an annual licence issued by the local Justices and at some considerable cost to the Drover.

This new ruling was to bring a dignity and reliability long overdue to this now lucrative business.

While holding this licence it was illegal to carry out the act of droving while under the influence of alcohol and in 1872 the fine for such an occurrence was 40 shillings or one month in gaol.

It was also a serious offence to move animals on the day of the Lord, the Sabbath. This carried a penalty of imprisonment and a substantial fine bringing disgrace and financial ruin to the perpetrator.

Because of these important changes in the profession, trust did survive the centuries and was to remain in the industry until the very end, which came in the 1850s. With the introduction of the steam trains. It was the iron horse that was to signal the demise of the droving trade. In 1922, there was a national rail strike and a few older characters thought there might be a chance of starting up the profession once again. They made it as far as Shrewsbury but were so tired, they called it a day. That was the very last attempt at using the old roads once again.

It had always been tradition that the Drover only paid the owner of the animals on his return. Because most of the Welsh were illiterate they could neither read nor write and could only speak the Welsh language each transaction was therefore recorded on a piece of paper by the drover with each droving family having its own motif a logo in today's language which was always in the shape of an animal and always in black. Some used sheep others horses others cattle, hens, pigs, rabbits, birds in fact any animal they could think of.

Every time the drover took animals on board he would draw the number, he received so that the supplier could instantly see the transaction. This record would be kept by the vendor and produced when eventually the drover made payment to him.

If it were one animal they would draw one, two a drawing of two and so on. A simple solution, which served its purpose.

Because of the poverty, prevailing throughout the whole of the Principality especially with those who relied on the land for living, money owed, was eagerly anticipated and gratefully received by those poverty-stricken farmers who were trying to make a meagre living under extremely difficult conditions.

More often than not, their only income for the year was from the sale of the one or two animals that they could afford to sell.

Others had to be kept to breed another generation.

There was always a saying amongst these farmers. Sell the best, but keep the very best.

Once the train started to take away business from the drover, it meant local farmers would now send their stock to local markets. Potential buyers would now travel by train from England to do the purchasing in Wales.

This new development meant animals could be sold locally and then taken to the local railway station loaded into specially built wagons and be transported over night arriving at the various destinations the following morning in relatively good condition not having lost up to thirty per cent of their body weight as they would have done during their three week journey by road.

The old ways of droving meant resting the animals once they arrived at their predetermined locations, which in the case of the Anglesey men were around the Chelmsford and Billericay areas.

One redeeming feature attached to these runts as they were called was that they put on weight very quickly so they would be ready to be driven on the final leg of their journey to Smithfield Market after about three weeks of grazing on the lush pastures of the London basin.

Many members of the public who lived within the confines of the city were fearful of these droves as many an innocent bystander suffered severe injuries, some even losing their lives as a result of these wild animals being driven at some speed through the crowded streets accompanied by shouts and cries in a language that was not understood by the English and was often referred to as the cry of a barbaric tribe.

6

Droving can be put into two classes. The long distance Drover and the short distance variety. Each one as important as the other. To describe this system. It can be likened to the veins of a leaf. The centre vein representing the long haul drove which is the one I am to describe in the chapters of this book and the smaller veins being the local droves.

The local Drovers would collect from various outlying farms and local markets within their area and meet the main drove at pre-determined points en route.

You can still find a corner of a field with a walled area close to a main thoroughfare often with Scot's pine trees still surrounding it. This is a certain indicator that the local drovers would have waited with their animals for the main drove to arrive. They knew that within two to three days, the big drove would arrive and the transfer of animals would be completed.

Days immediately prior to departure would have been full of vigorous activity for these cattlemen. They had to be more than well prepared for this arduous and more often than not perilous journey.

Well practiced in making the final arrangements successive generations had learned from bitter experience that lack of preparation could mean disaster and even loss of life.

Extra hands that were required would be selected for their experience and physical strength and would start arriving the day before departure.

The head Drover and owner of the operation would always have two trusted and experienced men along side him who would take up managerial positions and would be responsible for the smooth running and safety of the operation during the whole length of the journey.

Financial arrangements would be made and discussed carefully as they were forced to carry substantial sums of money to pay their dues on the journey and to settle affairs on behalf of others in the city of London.

Secret compartments were built into their saddles and their clothes. This was to conceal a substantial amount of gold coins that they would have to carry for the crown as they were entrusted with the collection of a Ship Tax. This was a tax paid if you owned a dwelling where you could see a ship at sea. All other coins would be carried in leather bags on either side of the saddles.

Always conscious of the threat of sickness and its effect on the progress of the drove they equipped themselves with what we would know today a first aid kit. This would contain various potions to cover most eventualities. These would be prepared by the local quack doctor who it seemed could cure all ills in both animals and humans.

One potion to survive to this day is Morris Evans's oil. This product you could drink, rub it on infections, oil hinges on doors and gates plus other applications too many to mention. It was truly miracle cure!

If any of the men suffered cuts to any part of their body then they would immediately encourage the dogs to lick the wound, as the saliva would act as an antiseptic speeding up recovery. The wound would then be covered with a hemp leaf and duly bound to keep out the dirt.

Goose grease and Bloneg (Pig Fat) would be carried in containers made from the trunk of the Elder tree. The Elder was very important to the drover as its many properties could be used in a multitude of different ways. Because the centre core is soft and full of pith, which is an excellent insulator, it meant the trunk could be easily hollowed out.

The small branches were made into musical whistles and flutes to be played on route and the lower part fashioned into containers. The branches are also a natural fly repellent, very useful when surrounded by cattle. A sprig was always worn on the front of the hat and the handles of the whips were made from this tree, as it was very light in weight but very strong. Another good reason for wearing a piece of elder was that it kept evil spirits at bay, proof that these tough men were also remarkably superstitious.

It was becoming more dangerous to travel as the years passed by and this meant that firearms were becoming an essential accessory.

Flintlock pistols were now part of their personal apparel carried and always pre primed ready to fire at a moments notice.

It was not uncommon to see six, three on either side pushed securely into the belt. The length of barrels on the front pistols would be two inches the next three inches and the ones at the rear in line with the hips four inches. This is probably is where the term six-gun came from.

Apart from fending off wolves, which were always trying to attack the herd it, was the highwaymen laying in wait over the English border that was the main reason for carrying such armaments.

As dawn broke over the majestic mountains of Snowdonia, it was time to leave. With goodbye's and best wishes exchanged, they were off on one of the most exciting and hopefully rewarding journeys of their lives.

The Anglesey breed of cattle is believed to be one of the oldest breeds in the United Kingdom, but were eventually crossed with stock from Caernarfonshire and Merioneth making them short in stature but with distinctive long horns that turned up at the ends and were known to the English as 'Welsh runts'.

Beef was very rarely eaten by the Welsh but was in great demand by the English. This is why there was a constant demand for the product, which proved to be a lucrative and important trade between the two countries for many centuries. Most of the armies were fed on this beef, as were most of the gentry of the land.

The drove would progress in an easterly direction each new meeting point producing more and more cattle, which then added to an ever-increasing total.

After crossing the island, the drover would soon be faced with the first and probably the biggest obstacle he would encounter on his long journey to London. It was the ferocious and extremely dangerous waters of the Menai' Straights, which happen to separate the Island from the mainland.

The waters of the Menai are amongst the most dangerous in the world and feared by the most experienced of sailors.

Long before that great civil engineer and constructor of bridges Thomas Telford was a twinkle in his Mothers eye getting off the island and onto the mainland had been a major problem for the islanders. Getting animals off was an additional headache.

Over the centuries these drovers had studied in great, detail the tides and conditions along the whole length of the straights. They were fortunate enough to meet and enlist the services of a local farmer who lived on the banks of the waters and who owned an old cow that would willingly enter the water without any difficulty. It is a known fact that if you can persuade one animal to enter the water others will inevitably follow. Needless to say, this shrewd operator made a small fortune hiring the same old cow every time a drove needed to cross. This valuable assistance was gratefully received as it saved valuable time and a lot of effort.

By studying the best spot to effect this major operation, they had made a decision to use a specific location at a place known as Gallows Point on the outskirts of Beaumaris on the North Eastern side of the Island.

The reason they chose this particular place is not too difficult to understand as it stands directly opposite the vast Aber sand banks and where the deep channel of water is at its narrowest.

It had been worked out that there was only a twenty minute window of opportunity for a successful crossing which meant forcing all the animals into the raging flow at exactly the right time, this being when the tide was turning and running to the North, this was the best and possibly the only chance they would have of making a successful and safe crossing.

Apart from anything else, it ensured that the animals were at least all going in the same direction. Once the last beast was in the water the men and dogs would cross in hollowed out tree trunks, which in fact were the earliest form of canoe.

The cattle and horses would be swept by the fierce currant onto the sand banks, their feet gradually griping the sand beneath them and eventually hauling themselves out of the water and onto the other side.

Richard Llwyd, on witnessing this event was motivated to write these lines.

> 'These are the features of the ferrying fair,
> And those who dote on discord may go there
> The tides, contending with the toiling boats,
> The horny forest that on Menai floats
> The brutes inferior, but by the windy storm,
> The living beach where bellowing droves depart,
> And the last low, that rends the suffering heart'.

Once safely on the other side and with a quick check to make sure they had all survived they then set off at great pace wading across the vast area of sand towards the coast at Aber. As far as we know, there were never any losses recorded whilst crossing this dangerous stretch of water.

Once on firm ground, they would make their way southeastwards heading for the mountain pass and the Roman road that would take them past the beautiful Aber falls then on to the difficult mountain path climbing between the summits of Foel Fras and Tal y Fan

At this point, they were to encounter a dramatic change in climatic conditions. The journey so far had been in the temperate climate of the Isle of Anglesey, which meant good visibility at all times, and reasonably dry weather.

Now it was to be different! Low thick cloud was to greet them, which meant very wet miserable conditions. This was a weather pattern, which was to prevail from here on until they arrived in the Vale of Clwyd some forty miles away.

Questions of how they coped must obviously be answered at this point. How did they overcome the problem of severe weather conditions? How did they navigate some of the roughest and toughest terrain in the country? How were they dressed for such an occasion? How did they survive?

There are many interesting answers to these questions. One of the first things they did was to make sure they were suitably dressed for the various conditions they would encounter. Equipping themselves with garments to keep them dry in heavy weather and cool on warmer drier days was of prime importance.

I would like to mention at this point that there are a series of links throughout this story.

They are, A house with a relatively unusual name (Buarthau). The finding of coins and artefacts underground. The Cowboys of America and Canada. Everest (The Mountain). The AA The motoring organisation not Alcoholic's Anonymous. Al Capone the gangster. No! He was not Welsh, or a Drover.

I have mentioned the first two. The house and the coins, the others will become obvious I hope as we proceed with the story. The link with the American cowboy starts with what they wore on their heads.

We know they wore a very wide brimmed hat of felt, made from mulching tree bark and mixing it with hemp. This was to keep the rainwater away from their shoulders as much as possible, very sensible!

They also wore a cape over the shoulders made from a mixture of welsh wool and hemp. Yes Hemp! A close relative to what we know today as cannabis. Whether they ever used this plant in any other way is not known. Who knows, if they did it may have made their journey a little more tolerable.

Their trousers were also made of a mixture of hemp and wool, again being very hardwearing and reasonably weatherproof. Braces held the trousers up and they also had the extra protection of heavy leather belts, which also served to hold their pistols in position.

Underwear was of pure wool allowing the body to breathe, this was important as garments were never changed from one day to another and washing the body was never often so to survive for three weeks or more their garments needed to be extra durable.

Clogs were worn on the feet with soles made from Alder; this being the only wood when wet never rots. Itinerants from the many groves that existed throughout North Wales centuries ago would harvest the clog bases.

Protection of their feet was of prime importance to these cattlemen. Three hundred miles of hard walking with any sort of foot disorder such as blisters could cause major upset and above all, delay.

To overcome this potential problem they greased their feet with fat known by the Welsh as bloneg, pig fat. Once this was done, they would pull on a pair of Welsh woollen stockings making sure they covered the knee and finally, the clog itself. By greasing the feet, it allowed the foot to slide freely within the clog eliminating friction, which would inevitably cause blisters to form on the skin.

The whole leg would then be covered with a type of brown paper again made from hemp and wood pulp then greased with animal fat and tied over the top with leather thongs.

This prevented water from entering below the knee and hopefully kept the feet dry. This could be likened to the modern day gaiter and later the Wellington.

It is because of this practice that we can today connect with the Everest Expedition of 1953. This very first team to successfully ascend the highest mountain in the world used the same technique of greasing the feet and wearing Welsh woollen stockings as the drovers had done for centuries. The only difference being they used boots instead of clogs.

It was probably during their training in the Mountains of Snowdonia, which I am told has a similar rock structure to the Himalayas that the Everest team comprising of Hillary, Sherpa Tensing and Dr Evans discovered this secret of protecting the feet from the dreaded blister by meeting the Snowdonia shepherds who use this technique even today.

This must have contributed greatly to the successful first climb to the summit of that great mountain.

One of many questions asked is.

How did these drovers navigate their way over great distances through the mists and low cloud?

They never carried maps and certainly never had the facility of satellite navigation to assist them but what they did have was a phenomenal memory, which helped a great deal. The accuracy of their navigational skills was viewed by many as a complete mystery but it was eventually solved,

They always planted a certain type of tree at strategic places on the route. Especially where there were very few features of identification to be found.

The special tree that they chose was the 'Scots Pine'.

Nobody really knows why they came to choose this species but it's a fair bet that it was because it grows straight, is relatively quick growing, lives for a long time and never looses its colour or its tassel's.

It is the only tree that can be seen clearly at a distance through the blankets of mist and cloud.

Today you can still find these trees on high ground often miles from villages towns or any form of habitation but it is always an indicator that the Drovers passed that way. These trees were planted at strategic places and at distances where each one could be seen from the other. Provided they kept one in sight, they knew they were safe to proceed with the herd to the next one.

It is a steep climb from the flats of Aber and these animals were new to each other. It would not take much to unsettle these nervous beasts and this could cause endless problems and definite loss. A stampede being one of their greatest concerns.

The head Drover would always ride on ahead to check on the safety aspect of the route and to warn stockholders that the drove was coming through, hoping they would have sufficient time to make sure any stray animals were put safely out of the way because if they accidentally joined the herd they would never be seen again.

This eventually led to the building of the 'Drovers Roads'. These roads were built to contain the drove and to keep all other animals at bay. All drovers' roads were constructed to a certain measurement. 12 feet wide, at the base with earth banks on either side. Hawthorn would be planted on the top or stone whichever was most readily available.

An interesting exercise can be carried out by anyone who can kneel or bend. If you make an effort to count the different species of plants contained within a square meter on the embankments you will find seven. These include grasses weeds and flowers. Each species represents one hundred years of existence a phenomenon nobody can really explain.

Therefore, we can assume the roads must have been put in around seven hundred years ago roughly the same time as the enclosure act.

The senior drovers were always mounted on sturdy horses. The lower and younger members of staff would have to walk with the animals. The horses used were the traditional Welsh Cob. A breed that has been in existence throughout the Principality since 1600 BC. Today this breed is in great demand throughout the world because of its unique characteristics.

It is the only horse that can be; Ridden, Carry weight, Pull large and heavy loads, Jump, Be placed in a harness and driven. Is very fast, sure footed and has great intelligence.

In the reign of Henry VIII, it was decreed, that every Welsh horse under 15 hands should be slaughtered. Because of the terrain and the agility of the animal together with its intimate knowledge of the mountains the breed evaded capture. Proud stallions with their mares were able to find hidden valleys and crags high in the mountains outmanoeuvring their pursuers.

Fortunately, the breed not only survived but also flourished.

From the small mountain ponies to the larger and more powerful Cob, the breed was to expand and become accepted throughout the world. The Cob because of its speed and sure footedness had been sought after to carry Knights into battle, Doctors to patients, Farmers to their stock, Bishops to their flocks and not forgetting the Drover to his destination.

Even the great Julius Caesar on seeing these magnificent animals realised their potential and the Romans in their great amphitheatres for chariot racing eventually used them.

As the Romans withdrew in 410AD it became obvious that the Cob had been crossed intentionally or otherwise with the Arab.

The Arab breed of horse had been brought over to Britain by the Romans from North Africa and the Cob of today carries certain characteristics of this breed, noticeably the head which has a bright eye dished nose leading to large nostrils very strong body and a positive carriage.

The Drover knew that in the Welsh Cob not only did he have a reliable means of transport but that at the end of the journey a valuable commodity to sell.

A constant steady pace was important to the Drover and an average two miles per hour was the speed they hoped to maintain throughout their journey which incidentally is the same calculation used by walkers today. Moving from dawn to dusk they were able to cover fifteen to twenty miles per day.

If the going one day was difficult and they lost time, they would try to make it up the next day.

That first day on the mainland was always a difficult one. Apart from negotiating rough mountain passes the poor weather and animals, having to get used to one another it was always fraught with stress

After the first steep climb to the top of the mountain range, it was a slow descent into the Conwy Valley and the crossing of the river Conwy at 'Tal y Cafn'.

It is here we first discover the name Halfpenny a 'Halfpenny Style.'

Wherever you see the name Halfpenny used such as Halfpenny lane Halfpenny Green and others, you will know with certainty that the Drovers passed that way as a halfpenny was for many years the standard charge per beast for overnight accommodation.

After spending the night on the banks of the river Conwy, resting and purchasing horses it was time to move the drove on.

Yet another climb from the valley floor over the wild moors of Hiraethog, passing the odd traveller on the way.

Stops were made at Gorse Mills high up on the moors.

These mills were always near to a fast running stream, as water was needed for the motive power to drive the primitive machinery used to bruise the gorse. Harvesting the gorse was a major undertaking and often carried out by children. It was only the young shoots that were of value the rest was discarded. Ground gorse was always in great demand by the drovers as fodder for their horses.

Bags would be purchased, transported and fed to their steeds as soon as they rested for the night.

As they reached the windswept moors, they were being forced to follow once again the drovers' roads. One of the reasons that these roads are to be found on high ground is because of the system the Welsh operated of summer grazing.

Most farms in Wales had a summer residence the 'Hafod' and a winter one known as the 'Hendre'. Hafod translated means summer dwelling, Hendre the old house, the lower dwelling. This meant that each year all the stock was transferred onto the hills in late spring where they would remain for the summer. This also meant that the whole family would follow living in the Hafod. This presented the drovers and the farmers with a problem as the original droving tracks went straight through their respective land areas. It was eventually sorted by the building of the roads. Sadly, most have been ploughed in by the Forestry Commission and are therefore lost forever, the remaining sections are sometimes difficult to find but there are one or two places where they can still be found.

As the sun became low in the sky on this section of the trip it would not be long before they had their first view of the Vale of Clwyd.

Surveying the land before them, they would have been aware of a complete change of scenery.

Below them was a very different landscape.

Gone the bleak marshy and desolate moor land with little or no vegetation apart from mountain grasses heather, gorse and of course, the odd Scots pine tree.

Now for as far as the eye could see, it was the canopy of a dense forest, a carpet of trees.

This would have been the scene over much of Britain for centuries as most of the country was heavily forested. It is said that a squirrel could jump into a tree in London and come all the way to North Wales without ever touching the ground.

The drovers as they descended to the valley floor were heading for the village of Rhewl and in particular a dwelling by the name of 'Buarthau'.

The reasons they chose this tiny hamlet were many and varied.

They knew it was relatively safe with a clearing made within the forest. An enclosure.

Protection during their weekend stay was paramount as there was a constant threat of attack by wolves and rustlers. Either could attack at any time during the hours of darkness and any losses would be costly to the drover not only in money terms but also in reputation.

Because an area had been cleared out of the forest and made safe and secure, it meant the young droving boys who were entrusted with the safety of the animals at all times, could patrol this area day and night with relative ease.

All animals need water and here they had the facility in abundance. The river Clywedog is almost level with the land at this point making it easy for the thirsty beasts to walk into the river and take on as much as they required.

Food for the cattle in the form of grass was readily available due to the excellent growing conditions within this part of the vale.

The journey they had just completed would have taken its toll on men and beasts as they had just completed the most difficult and strenuous section of their trip, if they had not achieved the two miles per hour up to this point then they would have to make it up from here on. It was customary that if the previous day had been hard and the pace slow, then they would make sure they made up for it the following day.

They would make sure that they arrived in Rhewl on a Friday evening, as they needed to utilise the whole of the weekend for various transactions. Apart from resting both men and cattle, the Sunday was definitely a day of rest as was mentioned previously any movement would evoke a serious fine equivalent in today's money of about £25,000. With automatic cessation of their licence.

7

With both runts and horses settled on the first night it was time for the men to relax.

The head Drover's all seemed to have the same weakness, they were serious gamblers and cock fighting their favourite sport. With one of the largest cockpits in Wales only a short distance away it proved to be a great incentive in choosing this particular spot for relaxation and recreation.

The Hawk and Buckle Inn in Denbigh now sadly no longer in existence was their target as it housed at the rear of the premises one of the largest cockpits in Wales. It was a cylindrical stone building with a thatched roof and capable of accommodating up to three hundred eager gamblers.

This building was moved stone by stone some years ago to take its place in the National History Museum of Wales at St. Fagan

It was some thirty feet in diameter with walls built of stone. There were large apertures in the stonework at regular intervals allowing light in and heat out.

In the centre was a raised circular dais about two feet from the ground. This was the centre of attention as it was the fighting ring.

Owners and trainers, would take up positions closest to their treasured birds with the punters standing on progressively raised areas around the interior allowing all a better view of this gruesome spectacle. Outside the building would be the cages containing the finest and most aggressive highly trained birds in the area.

Cockfighting was a regular event in the locality until it became illegal in 1849.but secret fights were still organised in various local villages within living memory.

Crowds would flock from miles around to their local pits be they indoor or out, all eager to witness gory encounters as these poor birds fought each other to the death.

Each village within the vale had its very own cockpit, some very simple basic affairs others more sophisticated but all well concealed. They even had portable ones that could quickly be moved from one location to another with lookouts posted at various points to warn if there was the smallest hint of the law approaching.

Each bird owner that participated in this barbaric sport had his own design of fighting spur. This was a metal spike sometimes in silver but mainly in sharpened steel, which was pushed crudely through a leather strap and then attached to the leg of the bird with leather thongs. These spurs were purposely designed to cause maximum damage to the opponent with every strike with the ultimate result of death.

The wings would be clipped making sure the bird stayed close to the ground and the beaks would be sharpened for maximum penetration. They were even fed a special diet of sweet butter with white sugar candy and rosemary or wheat meal mixed with ale and the whites of eggs. An alternative diet of wheat meal and bread soaked in urine proved on some occasions to be the winning formula.

The bouts could be riotous affairs often ending in pandemonium and fighting not just among the fighting cocks but also amongst the punters. With hundreds of pounds changing hands in one night and the drovers being probably the biggest spenders. I am sure the stress levels and tensions would be extremely high with all involved.

So sought after and treasured were the prizes that each owner would do virtually anything to make sure his bird was the best, the champion of champions.

8

When the first drove of the season was to arrive in the vale it created much excitement for miles around and it was eagerly looked forward to by the many local country folk who would stand to benefit from the various items they offered for sale to the drovers.

Others would travel miles just to be part of this annual experience as it was an important event of the calendar, it signalled the end of winter and the coming of summer, the long dark nights were now giving way to longer hours of light. Having an opportunity of meeting and talking to these drovers was an opportunity not to be missed; these were people from outside their own close community and who were able to contribute to their limited knowledge, informing them of what life was like over the border in England, its people and their customs.

They would also be fascinated by the countless experiences these men had encountered on their dangerous journeys south over the years.

The drover was well rewarded for his work, a weekly wage for the youngest drover was twice the going agricultural wage of the time and they were also paid a six-shilling bonus at the end of each trip when all the animals had been sold. This was in addition to the many deals they did every day by buying and selling virtually anything they could lay their hands on.

Their reputation for spending money freely was well known and that in turn attracted 'Ladies of the night' to their camp for the weekend.

These women would come to offer their services as companions for the night relieving these young men of their money and tension.

What a considerate group of ladies they were!

Because it was only the management that were allowed

accommodation and a roof over their heads at the Inns and ale houses, the younger men would have to bivouac around the perimeter of the enclosure.

I am sure not every night would have been spent worrying too much about the possible dangers that surrounded them. They would have relied heavily on the company of the ladies to help them cope with the loneliness and the cold during these hours of darkness.

It would also have been very odd if they had not found time to sample in some quantity the local ale while keeping a watchful eye on their charges.

Probably because they sampled too much of both, they happened to lose a substantial quantity of money from their pockets and pouches without ever knowing they had done so.

Because of this apparent carelessness or lack of concern, it meant these coins were to remain in the ground undiscovered for centuries until I came along with my metal detector.

9

Once the drove had entered the Vale no more cattle would be taken on board.

It is recorded that at this location in the early eighteen hundreds the largest drove ever recorded numbered in excess of a thousand animals with some fifty drovers in attendance. What a spectacular sight this must have been.

After Friday's activities had died down the Saturday morning would see vigorous activity by everyone as now many things needed to be done and jobs attended to with no time to waste.

One of the most important tasks was that all the cattle and the horses had to be shod, the reason being that ground conditions from now on would be so different. They would be using established tracks from here on, tracks that had been created through the forest and were now well used as thoroughfares with the earth having been compressed by constant use of carts, horse drawn wagons and stage coaches.

These roads were so very different to the soft boggy conditions that had been encountered over the past few days.

Wear and tear on the animals feet if not treated would be considerable and potentially disastrous as this would inevitably affect the condition of the beasts and reduce their pace. It is well known within the agricultural fraternity that if an animal suffers with its feet its condition deteriorates very quickly.

Because it was essential to protect the hooves of both cattle and horses from the rigours of these roads, it necessitated shoeing both the cattle and horses at this stage of the journey. The cattle required eight shoes to be fitted, two to each hoof owing to the cloven foot, the horses just four one for each hoof.

The demand for these metal shoes created by necessity, a number of farrier's who set themselves up within close proximity to the drovers routes. Each one producing many hundreds of pairs of cue's over the winter months ready for the spring and the many droves that took place during the season.

Nail makers would make nails for the shoes or cue's; these were very often Romany families that settled in close proximity to the farrier. The nails had to be made in their thousands bearing in mind there were at least five nails per shoe which meant forty per animal times one thousand for the largest drove which gives a total of forty thousand nails for one drove alone. These nails were more often than not stored in butter to save them going rusty.

Each farrier had his own pattern of 'cue' a family design that would be handed down from one generation to another.

The cue's were with some slight variations always in the form of two letter C's.

Some would have an added feature of a lip on the front of the cue. This could have the effect of stopping the shoe from slipping backwards which in turn eased pressure on the nails making sure the shoe would stay on longer. A travelling farrier was always taken on board at this point so that if a cue did become dislodged there was an instant replacement fitted.

It is recorded that one farrier and his young assistant could shoe well over a hundred beasts in a day. This operation needed to be carried out with precision and speed, as time wasted could not be regained during the remainder of the day. To accomplish this remarkable turnover, they used a long rope made of hemp and greased with pig fat, an eye would be woven at one end and the remainder of the rope would be threaded through to form a loop. The total length of rope could be as long as

thirty feet and when a beast had been selected from the bunch and with great skill the rope would be swung at speed around the head of the farrier and he would gradually release a small amount of rope with each circle until the loop became large enough to throw over the animal. When it dropped and came in line with the knees of the animal, the rope would be quickly pulled tightly around the legs causing the beast to lose its balance and fall to the ground it would then be wrapped tightly around the legs of the fallen beast with a knot. A stout branch measuring three feet with a fork at the upper end would then be placed so that the legs would rest within the fork. This would make it much easier to have complete control over the animal for the final fitting of the cues.

Where have we seen this practice of roping with a lasso before?

On the silver screen in the best cowboy films when they have to brand the young calves on the open prairie.

We in Wales have been using this technique for centuries, even long before Columbus discovered America.

Another activity to take place on the Saturday was the purchasing of various local commodities, not only for the trip but also to sell in the lucrative markets of England. This enhanced the drovers overall profits and contributed in no small way to their immense wealth.

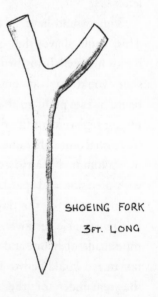

SHOEING FORK
3ft. LONG

One very special purchase they made during their stopover was woollen stockings produced by the men of Bala.

These unique Welshmen did more to contribute to the economy of Merionethshire than anyone could imagine.

Bala is known today for its lake, the deepest natural lake in Wales. What is not so well documented, is that the lake has been home to a very rare and elusive fish known as the Gwyniad (White fish). This is a deep- water species, which cannot be caught with rod and line but has to be trawled and was not known to exist until one was washed up on the shore of the lake after a major storm two centuries ago. Little is known of its habitat but it is said that it became landlocked during the ice age millions of years ago.

This beautiful and majestic scenic area of North Wales had suffered over the centuries from extreme poverty; there was little or no income as land was poor and non-productive. Local folks were surviving on what they could gather and what nature could supply.

The past had been very hard and the prospects for any sort of future was grim, but the people survived on their tremendous ingenuity. It was the men however, that found a part answer to this plight by becoming prolific knitters of Welsh woollen stockings.

The women folk made sure there was sufficient wool to keep production going. They were responsible for gathering and spinning the wool and would head up to the higher reaches gathering every strand of wool left by the sheep they could find, gorse bushes and sharp rocks proving to be a good source of supply. During different seasons of the year and if the supply of wool was poor, they would contract themselves as maids to the various farms in the area being paid for their services not in wages but in sacks of wool thus ensuring a sufficient supply to enable their the men folk to produce the final product in some considerable quantity.

It was normal for the women to carry all their loads on their heads. To do this, they had a circular hazel frame that would sit comfortably on the head; the load would then be placed on the frame and balanced. This was later covered with skin and a wide brim fitted which in turn kept the rain away from the shoulders. It eventually became known as the chimney hat that we see on many an old picture depicting Welsh ladies. They would often carry their baby on their backs wrapped in a Welsh woollen shawl; this meant they always had their hands free to carry out any task that was required.

During the long winter nights the womenfolk would sit in front of the peat fire spinning the wool, the men would be concentrating on knitting literally hundreds of pairs of stockings ready to sell to the drovers during their weekend stopovers in the vale of Clwyd.

It is said these enterprising men never stopped knitting day or night.

Even when they were participating in the most popular of pastimes drinking, they always kept production going.

They were able to achieve this remarkable production line because they had developed a technique that ensured speed and continuity, which was the envy of many.

Because they needed to knit on the move and to leave one hand completely free, they used a hazel stick cut to about two feet long with a metal spike the same diameter as a needle sticking out of the one end. The other end of this contraption was then thrust under the armpit and clamped securely against the body with the needle protruding from the other end. This was then used as the second needle or even a third which was essential for knitting stockings but it allowed the other hand to be free at all times.

A leather pouch was fastened to the belt, which contained two or more balls of homespun wool and was designed to allow free movement of the wool to the needles but more importantly, the free movement of the hand in guiding the tankard of ale to the mouth should they retire to a local hostelry.

The streets of Bala would be crowded on most nights, but Saturday night in particular with men knitting. They were known to walk up and down the streets of the town for hours sharing tales, experiences and with many a traditional song thrown in for good measure as they carried on their practice of producing their famous stockings.

The wives apart from making sure that their men folk had enough wool were also charged with the day-to-day running of the home, bringing up the children and very often looking after elderly parents.

Once March 1st, Saint David's day had passed, the men knew the drovers would soon be on their way and that they would arrive for the start of the season on the same weekend each year. Donkey's mules and horses would be loaded with hundreds of pairs of stockings together with bales of wool heading for their rendezvous. Raw welsh wool was in great demand by wig makers in London so in fact became an extra form of income.

It was a good days trek from Bala to Rhewl and they chose to follow the old Roman road passing the town of Corwen, the villages of Gwyddelwern, Bryn Saithmarchog, Pwll Glas and then finally on to Rhuthin. As soon as they arrived at their destination, they would make sure that their animals were fed and watered. The men themselves would bed down for the night, as they needed to be fully rested and alert for their dealings with the drovers in the morning.

Sales completed and the money safely in their saddlebags, the Bala men would then relax and involve themselves in the various activities on offer no doubt enjoying more than a pint or two of the local ale and contributing in no small way to the merriment of the evening.

Soon it would be time for them to return to the mountains. Men horses and donkeys would slowly make their way home to start the whole process all over again.

The stockings and wool once in the care of the drover would be carefully loaded onto wagons ready for the trip to London where there was a great demand for Welsh products by London society.

Other important purchases made by the drovers during this rest period were the locally made four wheel horse drawn wagons and two wheel traps and carts. Apart from being able to use these vehicles for transporting their purchases they were a valuable contribution to their overall profit as horses, carts and traps were in great demand in the city and would all command very high prices.

Denbighshire had its own cart and trap builders each with their very own individual designs. Apart from the skill of the maker, there was an abundance of the right timber close to hand. Wheelwrights were also close to hand as iron for the hoops was available from the Wrexham area some twenty miles away not too far away.

A particular design, which was much sought after, was the four-wheel wagon, which could be drawn by one horse or a team.

This vehicle had smaller wheels at the front with a bench seat for the driver and one other directly above an iron turntable that allowed the front wheels to steer. The remainder being an open flat space with sides capable of carrying large loads. Although light and easy to haul, it had great strength and durability.

These wagons could also be fitted with hazel hoops over the top, which could then be covered with animal skins, which protected the goods on board from the weather.

Again, we have seen this design used all over the world especially when needed to move heavy loads over long distances. It was probably the Welsh emigrant's who took with them this well and trusted design which in turn became known as the wagon of the West assisting the many pioneers as they carried their belongings to the new lands.

It is also interesting to note that local Denbighshire cart makers produced an unusual design of farm cart for land that was on a slope.

It had a single axle with one wheel larger than the other this meant if you were going across a sloping field the bed of the cart was always level. To turn around and come the other way, two pins were released and the body because it was on a turntable would be turned one hundred and eighty degrees with the horse still in the shafts. The pins would then be reinstalled thus allowing the vehicle to now travel in the opposite direction.

If you had a hill farm and most of them did, then this design must have solved a number of problems

10

Saturday night was always the main night for entertainment. Inns and alehouses would be set up for the traditional 'Noson Lawen'. (Night of Merriment).

This was always held in the largest building that could accommodate substantial numbers of people.

Apart from the many casual visitors, it needed to cater for musicians, dancers, poets, jugglers, magicians and especially Harpists as it was the harp that stirred the passion of the Welsh more than any other instrument. Originally, it would have been the traditional small Celtic variety that could be easily carried and played on the knee but it was the larger more impressive one that was to become the accepted instrument of the nation.

The triple row harp (Delyn Dair-rhes) became very special to the Welsh. Although imported into Wales in the 17th. Century it was soon to be adopted as the national instrument of Wales.

A difficult instrument to master as it has three separate rows of strings numbering in total 98. The outer rows represent the white keys on a piano and the centre row the black keys. The popularity of the harp in Wales can be attributed mainly to traditional 'Penillion'singing. This is a style unique to Wales where the singer sings one melody and the instrumentalist plays another but both hopefully finishing together at the end.

The most famous musicians of the eighteenth and nineteenth centuries in the area were a Romany family who travelled the whole of North and Mid Wales but eventually they settled in the Berwyn Mountains on the Denbighshire Merioneth border. Their surname was Woods. As is tradition in the Romany way of life, when the elder of the family dies he is always cremated his caravan burned and the remains of both are then scattered over the lands that they have adopted, in this case the Berwyn mountains, a true recognition of their affinity with this area over many years.

I have recently discovered a number of their descendants who have married and still live in the immediate locality.

Abraham Wood the founder first arrived in Mid Wales in 1730. His search for work on local farms brought him into North Wales.

This colourful and charismatic character was responsible for introducing the fiddle or violin into the traditional music scene and was much sought after as a skilled musician and storyteller.

He also became impressed with the Welsh triple harp so much so that he set out to learn and master it and eventually teaching his many children. Six of his sons became so proficient that they became much sought after in the many of the Alehouses Inns and homes throughout North Wales for their performing expertise especially during the nights of the Noson Lawen

The descendants of this masterful musician played a very important role in the development of traditional music throughout the United Kingdom.

One such descendent was later to be knighted for his contribution to classical music and he became, Sir Henry Wood the great conductor and composer of classical music and today is remembered by his annual Promenade Concerts performed each year at the Royal Albert Hall in London.

Abraham Wood died alone in a cowshed on the slopes of Cader Idris near Dolgellau. A sad end to a character that had given so much pleasure over the years.

As the last sounds of music laughter and verse filtered through the valley and the embers of the fire were starting to dim, thoughts would now turn to Sunday. This had to be a day of rest whether they liked it or not.

It was also a time to talk to the Lord and to ask for his guidance and safekeeping during the long days that were to follow.

On the strike of the midnight hour on Sunday night, the drove would to be made ready for an early start. As soon as dawn broke on the Monday morning instructions would be given to release the beasts from the holding pens and to keep them if possible in reasonable order as a stampede at this point could present major problems and major delay.

The head drover would set off some half an hour before the drove on horseback or sometimes in a new trap that had been recently purchased, ringing a bell and calling at the top of his voice two words not familiar to us, but according to professor Bowen of Aberystwyth University who is a leading linguistic expert they are the earliest cry known to man.

The two words were, 'Heiptri Ho'!

They don't mean anything to us but perhaps they did mean something to the cows.

However, if you listen carefully to farmers today calling in their cattle from the field for milking, there is an amazing resemblance to that original call.

There were very good reasons for the head of the drove to ride on ahead. One was to warn folks of the coming of the drove, the other to call the cattle that hopefully would follow.

Communication between the drovers was extremely important. They needed to tell each other what was required at all times but as you can imagine it was extremely difficult bearing in mind the distance between the beginning and the tail end of the drove. Some of the staff would be at the front, others along the right and left hand flanks and the remainder would be bringing up the rear. With all these animals on the move all getting used to their new shoes the noise must have been unbelievable and with the shear number of personnel involved, they didn't stand much of a chance of discussing anything. Shouting their instructions to each other would be futile, as they would never be heard so they needed to develop a system that would overcome this problem.

As they didn't have the luxury of mobile phones or the technology that we take for granted today, they did have their hands and it was the fingers that overcame this problem.

By putting two fingers under the tongue and blowing through them with some force it produces a unique frequency of sound that can be heard above anything else and by using a series of dots and dashes or short and long notes, they were able to indicate to the others their intensions.

Faster, slower, to the right, to the left, stop and start, each length of note meant a different command. This very effective method ensured that vital demands and commands were sent and received constantly making sure the cattle were kept in order throughout the trip.

We see the same technique used today by shepherds as they communicate with their dogs over long distances.

As they said farewell to the vale from this point there would be an addition to the staff in the form of a travelling farrier ready to swing into action at a moments notice.

Leaving the safety of the enclosures and the dwellings that had accommodated them over the weekend, it is worth a mention that it was not the Automobile Association as I thought that first introduced a method of displaying the quality of accommodation by symbols such as one, two or three stars.

The drovers had used a similar method centuries before but instead of stars; they used the familiar Scots pine tree to inform other travellers of the quality of the places to stay.

By planting one, two, or three, they were able to advise others of what they could expect. One tree being fair, two better and so on.

A number of Drover's Inns still have these trees in close proximity to the buildings even today. Yet another reminder of this sometimes forgotten part of history.

As the years went by and roads became busier, a new problem presented itself to the drover and that was the introduction of the turnpikes /tolls. Thomas Telford this time presented a problem to the drover as these tollgates were now being built at regular intervals and more often than not on the very roads, the drovers had used for centuries. This would mean extra expense, something they did not take too lightly.

Accommodation and overnight grazing was cost enough without having to pay to use the roads. These were canny men and were not prepared to pay for anything they didn't have to.

They chose to bypass these new obstacles but this meant loosing time and making the journey that much longer.

It is recorded however, that one Anglesey man left the drove and carried four of his compatriots on his shoulders so that he only had to pay for one pair of feet. They then rejoined the drove a little further down the road proving that these men did not spend money unnecessarily.

Leaving Ruthin and the vale they would then head for the villages of Llanarmon yn Ial and Llandegla. About seven miles in distance.

To reach these villages, they needed to veer off their original route and head North East once again climbing a fairly steep incline to reach these destinations.

The reason they made an extra effort to call upon these lonely communities was that Llanarmon and the surrounding area grew grain, wheat in particular. It was the only area in North Wales apart from Anglesey that could grow grain.

And the reason this area was so successful at growing crops was, the abundance of natural limestone rock.

The whole of this area is known today as the Happy Lands but was originally known as the Abbey Lands. These fertile acres were owned and farmed by the Cistercian monks of Valle Cruces Abbey in the vale of Llangollen.

This ancient order brought with them from Europe the knowledge and technique of burning limestone, which in turn was used on the land and then became the earliest form of fertilizer known in the British Isles. They were able to develop this area as there is a natural local supply of limestone from the rock structure that surrounds this area.

Although the land was relatively poor, it enabled them to grow substantial crops of wheat.

Some of the crop the monks would keep for their own use back at the Abbey and some they would use to fatten animals, the rest they would sell to the drovers.

With this abundance of grain naturally came alehouses. Some nineteen in Llanarmon and sixteen in the village of Llandegla. The monks also had their own brewery at the bottom of the horseshoe pass where the Britannia Inn now stands. Father Abbot would take up summer residence at a farm, which is called Hafod yr Abad, summer residence of the Abbot.

Because of this ample supply of grain, pigs were reared on a large scale and were often purchased from the monks by the drovers to be sold at the various markets which happened to be on route. One would assume that the pigs would be transported but this was not so, they were expected to walk, as there would be no room on board the heavily laden wagons.

To enable these pigs to walk and maintain a steady speed, they were muzzled to stop them grazing and their feet fitted with small bootees.

These would be made by local cobblers in the same way as a child's boot but much smaller they were made using an alder base with leather tops and lace holes all the way up to the top so that they could be fastened securely to the leg of the pig, fitting these booties was important if the condition of the animal was to be maintained during their long journey as once the feet deteriorate it causes distress and suffering to the animal resulting in severe loss of weight.

Once purchases had been made, they would set off to the next village Llandegla, here they would purchase geese. This was another animal that could be successfully bred and fattened with the abundance of grain.

To walk these poor birds any distance again would require protection to the feet and in this tiny village, there was the facility of a Goose bath. This was a rectangular indentation in the ground some twelve inches deep. At one end, hurdles were erected to contain the birds. The other end would have other hurdles that would guide these poor unsuspecting birds over crushed oyster shells and sand.

In the middle and on the side of the indentation there would be a pot of boiling pitch over an open fire.

On a given instruction, the boiling pitch would be poured into the indentation enough to cover the floor of the pit and the poor unsuspecting birds would be forced through it as speedily as possible.

Pitch hardens very quickly, so as they came out they would then tread on the shells and sand, both would quickly adhere to the feet and then form a hard pad enabling them to walk without suffering too much from wear and tear during the remainder of their journey.

A number of alehouses in and around Llandegla were constructed of peat blocks from the nearby bogs. 'Dafarn Dywyrch' means 'Turf Tavern'. Others on route were originally Tai un nos. These were dwellings built over night. 'Un nos' means one night. The law at that time stated that if you could build a house between the hours of sunset and have smoke coming out of the chimney by sunrise, then you could stake a claim on that piece of land. The boundary of the property was then defined by the throwing of an axe from each wall North South East and West and wherever it landed this determined the perimeter.

Many of these houses eventually became taverns and were frequently used by locals and travellers alike.

When all trading had taken place, the drove would leave the high grounds of the Llandegla moors, they would head for Bersham, and the crossing of the river Dee at Bangor is y Coed. Once over the border with England, they never purchased another item.

The problem from this point on the route was the constant threat of being robbed at gunpoint by highwaymen and rustlers who would lurk in the dense forests just waiting for the right opportunity to strike.

This meant keeping a watchful eye at all times by everyone.

A highwayman they frequently encountered while they were making their way through north Shropshire was Sir Humphrey Kynaston. He operated from a cave above Nescliffe near to the river Severn. His abode was within easy striking distance of a well-used thoroughfare linking the wealthy towns of Shrewsbury and Sweaty.

Kynaston was well aware that wealthy merchants constantly used this route so they became obvious targets. To launch an attack on the drover meant that he had to travel a little further to the North.

To have a titled highwayman was to say the least a little unusual. He had in fact originally inherited Myddle Castle from his parents, today it is a ruin that lies eight miles north of Shrewsbury but because of living well beyond his means, he found himself in serious debt and was eventually forced to relinquish his title and go into hiding.

The place he chose to live was just outside the village of Nescliffe.

A visit to the Three Pigeons Inn in this village will give an insight into the life of this well-known character as his story is well documented at this hostelry.

It tells of how he lived in his cave above the village and how he had a horse that when he whistled would come to him instantly. Then off they would both go to carry out their dastardly deed.

In reality, I think he became more of a friend than foe to the drovers as they sometimes willingly gave him such monies as they thought he needed to survive. It is said Kynaston was more interested in those wealthy merchants than the drovers and that he was more of a Robin Hood than a Highwayman, as he robbed the rich and gave most of his gains to the poor.

This is probably why this colourful character actually died of old age and probably penniless.

It was as they progressed towards the Midlands that things became more serious. Highwaymen became more aggressive and dangerous.

On one occasion the head drover who was some distance in front of the drove was suddenly stopped and money demanded by a masked misguided highwayman this unfortunate perpetrator was to loose his life very quickly. As the robber came close with pistol in hand demanding money the foot of the drover was out of the stirrup in the blink of an eye and was thrust into the man's chest forcing him to stumble backwards and as he did, was shot at close range through the head, never to rob again.

It became common knowledge that these Anglesey drovers were carrying substantial amounts of money in gold for the coffers of the Crown as payment of a ship tax.

I always thought you had to pay this tax if you owned a sea- going vessel but no, this was a tax levied on anyone in Wales who owned a dwelling where you could see a ship at sea from your front door, hence the name, 'Ship Tax'. The drovers were well paid on a commission basis for carrying out this dangerous task and this over the years contributed greatly to their overall wealth.

It was the cattle that was their most important cargo so important was the supply of Welsh cattle to the English Armies that in the mid 17th. Century, a letter was sent to Prince Rupert from the then Bishop of Bangor asking for a guaranteed safe passage for the Welsh Drovers into England as it could be likened to a Spanish Fleet, meaning presumably that the English could not do without the supply of meat and that its value must be equivalent to treasure.

From the North Midlands, they would meet up with other droves from different parts of the country, both Welsh and English; they then would share the route up to the London basin and would then split up and head off to the various grazing areas acquired by these men over the years. Today these grazing grounds are still owned by the descendents of those canny men If you happen to check the names of farmers and landowners in the Billericay and Chelmsford areas, you will come across the names of, Evans, Davies, Thomas, Williams, Jones, Harris and many others that are associated with Wales.

Once the tired herd reached these green and pleasant pastures, they would graze until they were ready for market. This could take up to three weeks. An impressive feature of these animals was that they put on weight very quickly, this being a great advantaged to the drover as they would have lost up to thirty per cent of their body weight on the journey.

On the hills of Wales, it is said, they could live on a ball of string but once you introduce them to grass, their weight gain was incredible.

The quicker they fattened, the better it was. It saved valuable time and meant the men could return to Wales and set up another lucrative drove immediately.

The more droves you could get in before the weather changed and winter looked like settling in the better. Once it was deemed the cattle were ready and fat enough, they would then be taken on their final journey into the centre of London, to be sold.

Local inhabitants often feared for their lives as these wild marauding beasts followed by equally wild Welshmen shouting at the tops of their voices in what appeared to be some sort of barbaric tongue which could not be understood by the locals were driven at some speed through the crowds, very often with serious consequences.

It was not unknown, for members of the public to be killed or severely injured during this practice.

When the final destination had been reached and the animals counted and sold, it was time to say goodbye to their dogs. Although these intelligent animals were of great assistance in herding on the long and arduous journey south they were very rarely appreciated by their owners and were treated with little respect and more often than not, cruelly. A pat on the back and the words 'Home' was enough. The dog was off.

These dogs had a homing instinct, which was unsurpassed. They would retrace their steps making for the Inns that they had stayed at on the way down. They would be given overnight accommodation fed, watered, and then sent on their way to the next Inn until they would eventually arrive home.

The North Wales dog was quite unique and very different to his counterpart in South Wales, which was the Pembrokeshire Corgi. This dog was small with short legs large muscles in the shoulder long nose and pointed ears, nearly always light brown in colour but extremely aggressive by nature. In fact a perfect design for a dog that needed to force animals in a forward direction by biting the ankles of animals and yet escaping without being kicked.

The North Wales breed was much larger almost the size of a goat but still sharing some similarities with the South Wales cattle dog.

Stiff upright ears long snout muscles on the shoulder but long strong legs and a long bushy tail. It was its colour and its outline that would eventually contribute to its demise.

A red brown coat with white under the chin and white belly made it easy prey to landowners who mistakenly took it for a fox and shot it.

The breed became virtually extinct but has recently had resurgence and is now to be seen around North Wales thanks to the few breeders who made great efforts to save and revive this rare breed.

The dogs would eventually arrive home some days before their owners which meant if the wives were up to no good!!! They knew that once the dog scratched the door the old man was on his way and everything had to be ship shape.

This remarkable ability of finding its way home whatever the conditions be it weather, raging rivers or the dangerous waters of the Menai Straights made this dog special.

I can confirm this instinct to be fact as when we farmed in the fifties we sold a sheepdog to a farmer in Gloucester as a result of an advert in a farming magazine.

On receiving the cheque, the dog was dispatched via train from Llangollen. This was an accepted mode of transport in those days and the dog was duly loaded into the guards van with the necessary food, water and labels.

Some weeks later, there was a scratching noise on the back door and when my mother opened it there was the dog. He had made it all the way back on his own. Needless to say we returned the money and kept the dog until he died of old age many years later.

Once the Welsh runts had been sold, the drovers would concentrate their efforts on selling their many and varied wares. This was extra income, cream on the milk so to speak.

The Welsh woollen stockings were always in great demand by the general public. Known for being hard wearing, warm in the winter, cool in the summer, they were most acceptable to high society and the ordinary city dwellers alike.

Wagons, traps and carts were also easily sold owing to their design and construction. Made of Welsh Oak and Ash, they guaranteed the purchaser a vehicle that would give long and trouble free service for many years.

Most of the horses would be sold and those that weren't would be ridden back to Wales to start yet another drove.

In the eighteenth century as more and more English gentry took over land in Wales, many needed to carry out transactions back in the city.

It was still a dangerous journey from Wales to the Metropolis and much feared by the 'would be traveller'. Therefore, it was decided because of the many dangers, to persuade the Drovers to carry out transactions on their behalf. As a result of this liaison, a new system of transacting business and handling finance over distance was invented.

The wealthy would hand over the required amount of cash needed to cover all their transactions in the City together with the various instructions. The drover would place it in safekeeping until his return.

When the cattle had been sold the cash received would then be used to pay the dues on behalf of the landowners as per their instructions. This eliminated the need to carry substantial extra cash on the journey.

We now see for the very first time, a transaction take place with just a piece of paper.

Because on the paper carried by the drover it had these words, 'I promise to pay the bearer'. Six words that have survived time and still remain on bank notes even to the present day. This was a major development in our history as now a piece of paper replaced coins.

It was the Welsh Drover therefore who invented and became heavily involved in the very first banking system in the world. This was to revolutionise the handling and carrying of money from one place to another forever.

From these humble beginnings, the drovers got their first taste of the world of finance. Their shrewdness, experience, knowledge, skills and excellent command of the English language meant they were in an ideal position to capitalise on a growing demand for money transactions and they soon became bankers in their own right, setting up special buildings for this purpose, giving their new banks names such as the 'Black Ox Bank' Banc yr Eidion Du, Black Bullock and many more.

As they became more sophisticated and the banking business grew, they often used their own names.

One such name that has survived all these years is Lloyds Bank, in Welsh, Llwyd. This particular bank was started by Samson Lloyd II in Birmingham in1765. Samson was originally an ironmaster but he even named a street in Birmingham with a welsh name, 'Dol bran street', Crow Paddock street; this was no doubt because of his family connection with Wales as his ancestors were all of droving stock.

The logo they adopted for the bank went back to those very early days of droving when his family must have used a black horse on their receipts. Today, that very logo is seen in nearly every high street throughout the length and breadth of Britain, it is the prancing black horse of Lloyds TSB. Although many takeovers and amalgamations have taken place over the years, the black horse has survived and is an important link with the days of old.

In the nineteenth century, members of the public would use the drovers as protectors and guardians if they wished to travel in relative safety from North Wales to the city of London. It was mentioned in some circles and by the sons of the wealthy wishing to return to and from society and city life, that the journey was akin to a grand tour to be much enjoyed.

Later, this experience became popular with many a young girl wishing to take up employment in service as there was a constant demand in the many large society houses in the city for maids and cooks.

These young ladies had been informed by the returning drovers of the substantial salaries being paid by the wealthy, wages they could only dream of back home in Wales.

It was some time during the mid eighteen hundreds that the Welsh took control over milk production and distribution within the city of London.

Many young women wishing to find a new horizon left the mountains of Wales to become milkmaids in London. With the drover being extremely shrewd and able to transact business in English and having the finance to develop various enterprises, he was bound to succeed in the milk business. Milking cows were placed all over London in purpose built milking sheds often behind shops. The milk was taken out onto the streets to sell twice a day by milk maids who would carry two tin pails attached to a wooden yolk worn across the shoulders each pail would weigh sixty five pounds and these young ladies would promenade up and down an area known as 'The milk walk'

In fact, every pint of milk sold within the city came from a Welsh company until eventually they lost overall control in the 1950s.

11

Once September arrived and the leaves were changing colour it was a sign that it was no longer advisable to attempt another drove for that year.

Weather conditions deteriorated quickly and made it almost impossible to make the journey without loss of life.

The extremely wet conditions would now give way to the heavy snows over the mainland. Mountain passes would become blocked, rivers would be frozen, and overall paths slippery with ice it was just not worth the risk. Therefore, the head drovers would now turn their attention to a different way of life becoming the newsmen of their day. They were much in demand all over North Wales at the winter 'Nosweithi Llawen' Merry Nights.

They would now be transformed into newscasters and became stars in their own right.

These winter nights of merriment would often be staged in the larger houses over North Wales. I was to find out that my step Grandmother was the daughter of 'Hafod Lom'. A traditional hill farm, now sadly lying silently under the dark peaty waters of Llyn Brenig to the North of Cerrig y Druidion. A reservoir supplying water to England.

Hafod Lom in its day, was one of the most important traditional farm houses in North Wales for it regularly hosted the winter version of the Noson Lawen. This was an impressive stone built farmhouse overlooking the scattered homes that surrounded the village of Pentrellyncymer and in an area where relics of Stone Age man have been discovered.

Its many rooms had large oak beams rooms and welcoming

fireplaces that were always fed with an endless supply of peat blocks harvested from the nearby bogs. It was also the home of a famous poet and drover Richard Morris who had taken time many years ago to pencil verse on a piece of plaster, which fortunately was carefully removed from the wall of the kitchen just before the waters were to drown this remarkable house forever. This fragment of history can be seen today at the Brenig visitor centre

Gathered around a blazing fire at 'Hafod Lom', dozens of people would listen to tales and stories related by the guest drover, he being the main attraction of the evening. For it was through his oratorical expertise that he informed the gathered throng of the latest news and new farming practices that were taking place over the border in England. It was he who would bring into Wales for the very first time cuttings of fruit trees, nuts, vegetables and other plants not known to Wales before, this was as a result of meetings with great horticulturalists such as Jethro Tull and others who themselves had learned of the new plants brought back from foreign lands. Seeds and cuttings of plants would be purchased by the drovers and then distributed free of charge to the appreciative audiences on these special occasions.

Wherever you see ancient fruit trees and bushes, surviving it is more than likely they would have been planted as a result of the seeds being given out free of charge by the drovers on one of these nights of merriment.

They would also inform the eagerly gathered crowd of the new lands that had been discovered across the sea in countries such as America, Canada, Australia and New Zealand.

The discovery of gold in the Yukon was available to anyone who could stake a claim and vast areas of land were being offered free of charge to anyone who could make the difficult and dangerous journey to the Wild West. Many great opportunities were waiting for anyone prepared to take the risk.

Audiences would be entranced by what they heard. These were a people who had never ventured more than a few miles from home throughout their lives and had no idea what lay beyond the nearest horizon, but here was someone they trusted relating stories of lands that offered great wealth, new lands that were waiting to be discovered with new opportunities and new hope.

The chance to make a new life.

For a people who were on the verge of starvation this must have sounded incredible and motivated many to consider leaving their native land forever.

The pocket-sized parcels of land that families were desperately trying to work were being further reduced in size every time the head of the family died. This was because throughout Wales a system known as Gavelkind was the accepted system of hereditary distribution. This is when on the death of the elder in family the males share the area of land equally, therefore eventually making their land area smaller with each generation and rendering it almost worthless.

England had abandoned this practice and instead adopted a system where the eldest son inherited the land in total therefore maintaining the whole farm and ensuring the future of the enterprise, giving the recipient a reasonable chance of making a living. It was however not very fair on the remainder of the sons in the family as they often had to leave home to find employment elsewhere.

It was the information that was relayed on these nights, which eventually brought about a mass exodus of young males and fuelled emigration in the nineteenth century, which has been unequalled since.

These young men had been born and bred on the land and they knew all there was to know about the welfare of animals, they were experienced horsemen and cattlemen they were able to survive the elements, they were tough and ambitious, all they wanted was something better than they had and that wouldn't be too difficult.

These were the young men who would join the drove the following year and were always welcomed by the drove master as he was aware of their great knowledge and experience. On reaching London and having collected their wages, they would say a final farewell to their friends boarding ships heading for the new lands in search of fortune knowing well that they would probably never see this country again.

When we read or see the films about the cowboys of the Americas, we know that it's a fare bet that most of them came via the droving stock of the United Kingdom. The only difference being, they would now be herding cattle over thousands of miles where as in Britain it was only over a few hundred.

For thousands of years the Welsh had never ventured very far, they had stayed close to the family unit, marrying within the community, bringing up their children and in the end being buried in the local cemetery. When it came time for these sons to leave Wales and say their final goodbye's to their families it must have been one of the most traumatic and sad experiences one could ever imagine.

Those poor Mothers and Fathers sisters and sweethearts would know well, that the chances of seeing their children ever again were extremely slim.

12

It is to one of those droving sons of Wales that we turn to for our connection to Al Capone.

Al 'Scarface' Capone was not Welsh, but the head of one of the most famous gangs America has ever seen. His right hand in the operation was a certain gentleman called 'Lew the Hump' and it was he, who did much to keep Capone out of prison throughout his life of crime.

Lew's real name was Llewellyn Morris Humphreys the eldest son of a Brian and Ann Humphreys who emigrated from a small farm in the mountains above Carno in Powys. He got his new name because there wasn't one person who could pronounce Llewellyn or Humphreys, so the first four letters of both the Christian and surname were used.

Llewellyn's Father Brian had been a drover back home in his native land but had found it difficult to survive with a young bride and a young family.

He decided to try his luck in the new lands of America having been made aware of the immense wealth that was readily available to the new breed of pioneer. The poverty and financial pressure that was being exerted by the new English landlords forced many a family to emigrate and the Humphreys family took up the challenge and headed for Chicago.

Known as the windy city it had for many years been the place where cattle had been driven over land for thousands of miles from the wide-open spaces of the west to the acres of holding pens built by the railroad company. From here, they would be transported on the remainder of the journey by train to the markets of the east.

Sadly, Brian Humphreys soon fell for the low life of drink and gambling, riding the range became the last thing on his mind and it was his young son who was forced to find employment so that the family could eat, hold together and survive.

At the age of seven, he became a newsboy selling papers on the dangerous street corners of this volatile and violent city.

Growing up very quickly and being the only breadwinner, it did not take long for the young Llewellyn to fall foul of the law. He was to end up in the local court at the age of thirteen.

The court judge on that occasion was a Jack Murray a man with Scottish connections. He was so impressed with the young boy in the way he conducted his own defence and with his impeccable manners his dress, and polite demeanour that he took to the young Llewellyn immediately. This was to change this young boy's life forever because as time went by he became a virtual son to the judge and his family. Jack Murray made sure from that day in court that this young boy had the finest education money could buy.

He took to education very quickly and progressed through the process of learning with great speed eventually passing out with the highest of qualifications. He had a leaning for the law and studied every aspect in detail eventually gaining qualifications that were to introduce him to the higher society of the legal profession. This however did not take him out of the world of crime but gave him extra knowledge of the law and the way it could be manipulated in a City that was controlled from top to bottom by gangsters and the mob's.

This was the era of prohibition and of vast sums of money earned illicitly.

It did not take long for the young Llewellyn to become a major player and to become involved with public enemy No 1 in America, Alfonso 'scarface' Capone.

Rising through the ranks of the mob quickly Capone became reliant on him as he was a thinker and way ahead of his contemporaries.

He eventually married a young girl who was half Native American

Indian and half Irish. She was the only female ever allowed into the inner sanctum of the mob as she was extremely bright and had a phenomenal memory. She never committed anything to paper, which meant there were very few records kept.

They had one child, a girl and they named her Llewella maintaining the Welsh connection.

Al Capone had been the most famous gangster in American history involved in anything and everything from Bootlegging in the days of prohibition to protection, bank robberies, murders and above all controlling the politicians in this corrupt city. Capone was eventually captured and imprisoned but only ever charged with tax evasion. This lesser conviction was as a result of the skills of a Llewellyn Morris Humphreys. He became known by the Capone outfit as 'Lew the Hump' Capone having difficulty pronouncing the Welsh names called him Lew instead of Llewellyn and Hump instead of Humphreys.

However, once Al Capone was off the scene, Lew took over the outfit and soon looked for new ways to make the activities of the mob look more acceptable. He laundered the profits would you believe through a massive laundry business that he purchased and started to look for a more respectable way of investing the many millions of dollars the gang and he had amassed.

Investing most of the money in the entertainment business. He was the first to open a hotel and casino in the desert of Las Vegas and put large amounts of cash into the world of cinematography because this had been his hobby ever since he was a young boy.

Lew controlled the purse strings in every major film studio in the United States, Warner Bros., M.G.M., Universal Studios, Pathe News and many more smaller companies all over the United States of America. Every famous actor and actress throughout the 1940s and 50s was in the employ of this Welshman.

Over the years, his ability to outperform the legal profession had now made him public enemy No 1 but he was able to secretly leave

America and in 1963 came back to Wales for the very first time since he left as a young boy. He brought with him his wife and young daughter. His search was for the old home a small holding called Castell translated into English, 'Castle' not that it was or had been anything like a castle, the only connection it may have had was that it stood on top of a hill, high up on the mountain above Carno in Montgomeryshire.

Now, it was little more than a ruin but still farmed. The house was much as it was all those years ago but the buildings had suffered from lack of investment and were now in a sorry state. The land was still as poor as it always had been; walls and fences had taken their toll from the extreme weather conditions that can prevail at these altitudes. In all it was a sad sight but faint childhood, memories started returning. One experience he had never forgotten and which proved that it must have left an overriding impression on the young Llewellyn was the day the family left the house for the last time with the final goodbye's to Grandparents friends neighbours and other members of the community. They were off to try a new life in that great land known as America.

His old home was one of a number of small hill farms on an estate, which was now owned by a wealthy businessman residing in London. The farms that were still trying to make a meagre living were finding it difficult to survive as rents were being forced higher and higher while incomes remained small.

Each quarter day, this being the day when the rents for these farms were due to be paid all the tenants would make their way to a local Solicitors office in the town of Llanidloes. Most of the families finding it extremely difficult to scrape enough money together to pay these ever-increasing dues and most likely had to go into debt to pay them.

Nevertheless, the outcome this one day in 1965 was to be different.

Each tenant in turn was escorted into the inner office by the secretary, but on entering the dated room surrounded by volumes of dusty legal documents that seemed to have been there for generations and which cast an almost depressing shadow on the room. This time the solicitor had a very different task to perform. Looking over his half rimmed glasses and with a wry smile, he refused to take any payment but instead handed each attending tenant a large official looking sealed brown envelope with each recipients name and address typed neatly on the front.

Many a heart must have missed a beat that day, as it was not uncommon for a 'Notice to quit' to be issued without warning or reason. Families could be turned out of their properties at a minutes notice with nowhere to go resulting in disastrous consequences. On this occasion, when the envelope was opened it contained the biggest surprise of all.

It held the legal deeds and documents of transfer to each of the present tenants' property in their names. All that was needed now was their signature on the bottom of the document.

The infamous Llewellyn (Murray) Morris Humphreys had purchased the whole estate after his visit to his family home in 1963 and had given instructions that the ownership of the farms be transferred to the people who were now working the land. From that very special day, the farm and the land was now theirs to work as they wished. Ownership was back in the hands of the Welsh free of debt and charge. Whether the money used for the purchase had any connection with the ill- gotten gains of the Al Capone's empire we will never know and I am sure not too many will even care.

The Murray in his name had been taken from his adopted Father, 'Murray the Judge'. It was he who had guided this Welshman to become the most influential and some say the most infamous character in American history from the 1930's through to the 1960'.

There is little doubt that this fascinating man will be remembered by many down through the ages of time.

13

The story of the Welsh Cattle Drover is a fascinating one. The Anglesey Drover a unique one. The practice of droving had gone on for a thousand years uninterrupted and only ceased when the steam trains started to penetrate the valleys.

When I was seventeen my very first paid job after leaving school was driving a livestock lorry collecting animals from outlying farms and delivering them to the local markets. These were the very markets that I had attended as a young child and had enjoyed so much. The wheel of life had turned full circle. Here I was once again back in the same old surroundings. Sadly the old characters had gone but a new generation had taken their place and most of them looked quite similar to the old boys still with their weather beaten heavily lined faces but now they had adopted a new habit, gone were the clay pipes and the chewing of tobacco They were now smoking posh ready rolled cigarettes.

The motor lorry had now replaced the train. Road transport was faster and more convenient. Maybe as the roads are too congested and Governments give incentives for alternative methods of transport the railway may come back into its own, who knows? There is one thing certain however; I do not think we will ever see the return of the long distance Cattle Drove ever again.

How strange life is, that after all the years, I once again became involved in the business of moving animals to market.

There were only a few families ever involved in Droving. It was always described as an art and a craft that was guarded from outsiders and handed down carefully from one generation to another. We as the Welshmen and Women of today owe so much to the so few. These characters were outstanding contributors in so many ways to the development of Wales, its customs and its people. I only hope that within these pages I have been able to give a small insight into their remarkable lives.

All I can say to these men as I draw this story to a close is,

On behalf of us all, we the people of Wales have the privilege of treading the paths and sharing the views and history of this unique, ancient, green and very pleasant land.

Thank you very much.

Diolch yn fawr iawn.